D0408285

GIFT OF THE
CLAYTON COMMUNITY
LIBRARY FOUNDATION

CLAYTON

"For me to offer the world instruction about prayer would be impudence."

C. S. LEWIS

CLAYTON

InterVarsity Press books

by James Emery White

Embracing the Mysterious God

Serious Times

The Prayer
God Longs For

JAMES EMERY WHITE

CONTRA COSTA COUNTY LIBRARY

3 1901 03837 9527

InterVarsity Press
P.O. Box 1400, Downers Grove, IL 60515-1426
World Wide Web: www.ivpress.com
E-mail: mail@ivpress.com

©2005 by James Emery White

All rights reserved. No part of this book may be reproduced in any form without written permission from
InterVarsity Press.

InterVarsity Press® is the book-publishing division of InterVarsity Christian Fellowship/USA®, a student
movement active on campus at hundreds of universities, colleges and schools of nursing in the United States
of America, and a member movement of the International Fellowship of Evangelical Students. For
information about local and regional activities, write Public Relations Dept., InterVarsity Christian
Fellowship/USA, 6400 Schroeder Rd., P.O. Box 7895, Madison, WI 53707-7895, or visit the IVCF website
at <www.intervarsity.org>.

All Scripture quotations, unless otherwise indicated, are taken from the Holy Bible, New International
Version®. NIV®. Copyright ©1973, 1978, 1984 by International Bible Society. Used by permission of
Zondervan Publishing House. All rights reserved.

With permission from InterVarsity Press, portions of chapter eight have been adapted and enlarged from
Embracing the Mysterious God ©2003 by James Emery White.

Design: Cindy Kiple
Images: Teri Dixon/Getty Images
ISBN 0-8308-3327-7
Printed in Canada ∞

Library of Congress Cataloging-in-Publication Data

White, James Emery, 1961-
  The prayer God longs for / James Emery White.
      p. cm.
  Includes bibliographical references.
  ISBN 0-8308-3327-7 (cloth: alk. paper)
  1. Lord's prayer—Criticism, interpretation, etc. 2. Spiritual
life—Christianity. I. Title.
  BV230.W48 2005
  226.9'606—dc22
                                                                                          2005004489

P	17	16	15	14	13	12	11	10	9	8	7	6	5	4	3	2	1
Y	17	16	15	14	13	12	11	10	09	08	07		06		05		

Contents

Acknowledgments

*T*o my wife, Susan, who continues to make every page of every book possible. To my four children—Rebecca, Rachel, Jonathan and Zachary—who have endured living with an author for a father their entire life.

To Cindy Bunch, who has been an advocate for my writing for several years now, and through that advocacy continues to give the most trenchant of advice, while leaving room for me to follow my heart.

To Jeff Crosby, Krista Carnet, Andrew Bronson and Brooke Nolen, who continue their ministry of making books like this one known. Thanks.

Finally, heartfelt gratitude to E. Glenn Hinson, who as a seminary professor first introduced me to the classics of Christian devotion nearly twenty years ago. More to the point, he was the only professor who took the time to try to teach his students how to pray.

Introduction

The Prayer We Long For

"Prayer lives among us as a wraith of what it was."

Karl Rahner

Questions. Our lives are filled with them. And many of them, particularly the ones we ask of God, go unanswered. It's not that they are unimportant to him; they are *terribly* important to him. It's just that *we* are even more important, and he is waiting for us to ask the right ones. The New Testament is filled with such misdirected requests—"Show us the Father," "Save us!" and "Who among us is the greatest?"—that Jesus declines to answer, opting instead to reveal more intimate, more significant insight into the character of God.

But one question was answered—immediately, clearly and with care.

"Teach us to pray!" (Luke 11:1).

They'd finally asked the right question.

The breath of spiritual life is prayer. Physically, we can live forty days without food and three days without water, but only seconds without breathing. Spiritually, we can do no better. A life without prayer cannot be spiritually alive, no matter what else may be present. It is, as Evelyn Underhill has written, "breathing the air of eternity." This is how strategic and critical prayer is for anyone who desires to be in a personal relationship with the living God.

And there is a *specific* prayer God wants to hear and we most need to express. It is not the prayer that makes us feel a certain way or that attempts to gain a particular advantage. It is the prayer that seeks out God and then experiences him. This experience is supernatural and, yes, mystical, but not in the way most would think. When we pray, we open the inner recesses of our life to the stirrings of God. There his transformational energies are released, and Spirit encounters spirit. As Moses maintained, "the LORD our God comes near when we pray to him" (Deuteronomy 4:7 NCV). And he knew. The Bible tells us that "The LORD would speak to Moses face to face, as a man speaks with his friend" (Exodus 33:11).

So prayer is not simply a matter of words but also relationship. This does not make prayer easier but more complex. If it was simply about skill or exact verbiage or words, then prayer could be approached as a competence to be mastered. Instead, it is deep calling to deep. For this reason the disciples implored Jesus, "teach us how to pray" (Luke 11:1). They had the rote formulas and pat routines; they knew of the times and patterns, postures and positions. They were interested in how they might relate to the living God the way Jesus did. So they asked Jesus to teach them how to have the relationship with God through prayer they saw Jesus enjoy.

But there was more behind this request. Religious groups and sects were often marked by how they prayed. Almost as if a denominational distinctive, how you prayed defined your religious identity. The disciples wanted to know what the defining prayer for their band would be (which is why this prayer is best termed the *disciple's* prayer rather than the *Lord's* prayer; for the true Lord's prayer, see John 17). Intriguingly, Jesus did not say, "You will not be known by a prayer." Instead, his answer suggested, "Here is the prayer that will mark *you*." And it would define them. Authentic prayer is deeply molding and transforming, making its content decisive for the life of the Christian. The Latin tag *lex orandi, lex credendi* (literally, "law of praying, law of believing") suggests that what is prayed indicates what may be believed, and conversely, what is believed should govern what may be prayed. No wonder that the early church considered the import of the Lord's Prayer to be second only to the Lord's Supper, and one of the most precious possessions of the Christian to steward, taught only to converts at baptism.

Yet somehow we have lost this knowledge, or lost touch with its importance. Some of us never had it, coming to faith in Christ late in life without a spiritual heritage or memory to draw from. Others have lost the deep meaning of Christ's words; even among those who recite it as a part of their weekly worship, the words have often become a matter of rote recitation or liturgical comfort. We need to return to Jesus and ask what his original followers asked: Teach us to pray.

Because we don't know how.

My church occasionally develops its weekend services by asking people to submit their top spiritual questions. The leading topics become series with titles such as "You Asked for It" and "My Big Question." No matter how many times we have offered people the opportunity to submit their leading questions, the most founda-tional issues related to prayer continue to make their way into the vanguard of concerns. Here is a sampling of the questions during one of the more recent polls, offered exactly as submitted:

- When a group is asked to pray for someone, why is this??? . . . 10 prayers needed for a small thing. 1000 or more for serious things such as cancer??? Signed VERY CONFUSED.

- Who has the "hot line"? . . . Is . . . God political? Does the most prayers win?

- Do you pray to God or Jesus or both?

- How should a person pray? Is there any special way to pray?

- Since God knows everything, why do we need to pray and ask for things?

- Is it okay to ask for specific needs or do I need to ask for wis-dom? Will God be interested in specific wants?

So we turn to Jesus for answers and find that he does not suggest that there is a particular place to pray, much less a direction to face. There is no mention of a specific day or time. Jesus does not consider important what a person wears while praying. He does not say anything about whether we should stand or sit, kneel or lie down. He never communicates whether we should close our eyes, talk in our head or speak out loud. Apparently, none of this is important to the prayer God wants.

Here is what Jesus taught:

This, then, is how you should pray:
"Our Father in heaven,
hallowed be your name,
your kingdom come,
your will be done
on earth as it is in heaven.
Give us today our daily bread.
Forgive us our debts,
as we also have forgiven our debtors.
And lead us not into temptation,
but deliver us from the evil one." (Matthew 6:9-13)[*]

The *Pater Noster* (Latin for "Our Father"), as it was referred to

---

[*] The traditional ending ("for yours is the kingdom and the power and the glory forever. Amen") did not appear in Matthew's original text as evidenced by the earliest manuscripts, though it did appear as early as the *Didache,* a second-century manual on morals and church practice.

for centuries, was no formula, much less a magical incantation that was to be repeated word for word. Jesus' teaching on prayer was a road map for the journey of seeking the face of God. While praying the Lord's Prayer verbatim has a rich historic and liturgical tradition, and it has its place in the life of any believer, the words speak most directly to the *kind* of prayer that should be offered and how we should be *when* we pray. They reveal the prayer and, more important, the pray-er, God wants.

The corporate dynamic inherent within "Our Father," while rich and worthy of exploration, cannot be engaged apart from a personal, private grasp of its immediate application to us as individuals. "Again and again in public and private devotion the Lord's Prayer is taken on hurried lips, and recited at a pace which makes impossible any realization of its tremendous claims and profound demands," writes Evelyn Underhill. "Far better than this cheapening of the awful power of prayer was the practice of the old woman described by St. Teresa, who spent an hour over the first two words, absorbed in reverence and love." And there is much to absorb. Tertullian (c. A.D. 160-c. 225), offering the earliest known discussion of the prayer outside of the Bible, called it the "epitome of the whole Gospel," and Augustine called it the source of all others prayers. No wonder Thomas Merton wrote that "Saying the *Pater Noster* is like swimming in the heart of the sun."

But many of us do not know how to swim. So we begin with a

tentative foot in the water, testing the temperature, penetrating the surface in order to cast ourselves from the shore. The first lesson seems simple enough; we just say, "Our Father."

ONE

Intimate

"Our Father"

The most basic question when it comes to prayer is to *whom* do we pray? This question comes up with surprising frequency, even among my seminary students, because we are not quite sure how to address a triune Being. Of course, we worship all three persons of the Trinity. British author and preacher John Stott is reported to begin his time of prayer each morning with an intentional effort to worship God in all of his triunity, declaring:

> Good morning, heavenly Father; good morning, Lord Jesus; good morning, Holy Spirit. Heavenly Father, I worship you as the Creator and Sustainer of the universe. Lord Jesus, I worship you, Savior and Lord of the world. Holy Spirit, I worship you, Sanctifier of the people of God. Glory to the Father, and to the Son, and to the Holy Spirit. As it was in the beginning, is now, and will be forever. Amen.

Stott, in his trinitarian worship, is on to something. God is three persons who are one God; yet are we to pray to all three? Jesus, who is God the Son, begins his instruction by telling us that we are to pray to God the Father. But giving us this instruction reminds us that we can *only* pray in Jesus' name. It is our relationship with Jesus that gives us access to God the Father. While each prayer is made to the Father, it is prayed in the name of the Son—meaning in the context and reality of a relationship with Christ. He is the one who brings us home, makes the introductions and provides the basis for the relationship. This reality was so apparent to the early disciples that at times they prayed directly to Jesus (Acts 7:59; 2 Corinthians 12:8), but these seemed exceptions to the rule: prayer is properly addressed to God the Father.

Yet prayer is still deeply trinitarian in nature; we pray to God the Father in the name of the Son and *through* the Holy Spirit. There is no instance in the New Testament of prayer being addressed directly to the Holy Spirit, perhaps because while the Father is in heaven (Matthew 6:9) and the Son sits at his right hand (Romans 8:34), the Spirit is with all Christians (John 14:16-17). Yet we cannot pray *apart* from the Holy Spirit. This was Paul's reminder in his manifesto to the Roman church, stating that the Spirit helps us in our weakness.

We do not know what we ought to pray for, but the Spirit himself intercedes for us with groans that words cannot express. And he who searches our hearts knows the mind of the Spirit, because the Spirit intercedes for the saints in accordance with God's will. (Romans 8:26-27)

So Jesus begins by encouraging us to address our prayers to God the Father, which later Christians would understand to be in the name of Jesus through the mediating work of the Holy Spirit. It should not surprise us that when we enter into communion and conversation with the living God, it would be as communal in nature as *his* nature is.

Even though they had yet to be introduced to the mysteries of the Trinity, or at least had yet to grasp it, properly designating God as *Father* would not have been startling to Jesus' listeners. *Addressing* God as Father was another matter, for while it may have been understood by a Jewish person that God *was* Father, to *call* him that to his face would have been considered a bit cheeky. Yet this is precisely what Jesus taught them to do.

And not just any term for Father.

The most startling word on prayer from Jesus' mouth was the term he encouraged his disciples to use to address the paternal side of God. As the research of Joachim Jeremias concludes, "all . . . strata of the Gospel tradition report unanimously and without any hesitation that Jesus constantly addressed God as 'my Father' . . . and show that in so doing he used the Aramaic form aba [Abba]." Jeremias adds, "We are thus confronted with a fact of the utmost significance. Whereas there is not a single instance of God being addressed as Abba in the literature of Jewish prayer, Jesus always addressed him in this way." That this was passed on to the disciples as the model for prayer is found in the use of *Abba* throughout the New Testament, demonstrating that the idea shaped the deepest levels of their thinking. "For you did not receive a spirit that makes you a slave again to fear, but you received the Spirit of sonship," wrote Paul to the Romans. "And by him we cry, '*Abba*, Father'" (Romans 8:15). To the Galatians, Paul wrote, "Because you are sons, God sent the Spirit of his Son into our hearts, the Spirit who calls out, '*Abba*, Father'" (Galatians 4:6).

Why does this stand out? For the same reason it does today.

Abba was an intimate term that would be used in families between small children and their fathers. The Talmud states, "When a child experiences the taste of wheat [i.e., when the child is weaned], it learns to say *abba* and *imma* ['dear father' and 'dear mother']." *Abba* and *imma* are the first sounds from a child's mouth, and while often used by adults toward their parents as a term of endearment, it remained children's speech. In contemporary English it has often been suggested that *Daddy* or *Da-da* would be much closer to the spirit of "Abba" than *Father.* This was not a stiff, solemn address but a term of endearment spoken with the affection and intimacy only a young child could bring to its saying.

So how should we pray? *Intimately,* as if we are crawling into the lap of our father, feeling his loving arms wrap around us as we

share the intricacies of our lives; not childish in the sense of immaturity or in the sense of meaningless chatter, but childlike in the
sense of the relationship itself. When a child talks to a parent, at
least in a healthy parent-child relationship, there is disarming
honesty, an absence of guile, utter transparency, boundless affection, unquenchable curiosity and absolute truth. It is not surprising that early Christian liturgies prefaced the Lord's Prayer with the
words, "We make _bold_ to say, 'Our Father.'" Or as Augustine observed, the Lord's Prayer is something we "dare" to say (_audemus
quotidie dicere_).

And addressing God this way _does_ take a sense of daring.

Back when my daughters were young, when I would come
home at the end of a day, they would first want to tell me all about
theirs, and then they wanted to play with me. Often, this meant
fixing my hair. They wanted to put me in rollers, create braids, put
in bows and pins. It goes without saying that doing this to me
would not have entered anyone else's mind. That kind of intimate
interaction could only occur between a father and his daughters.
As they worked, they were in heaven. Or perhaps given a picture
of it, along the lines of Susan and Lucy in C. S. Lewis's _The Lion, the
Witch and the Wardrobe,_ rolling in the grass with Aslan following his
resurrection "so that all three of them rolled over together in a
happy laughing heap of fur and arms and legs."

This is not the way those who first heard Jesus' teaching had
been taught to pray. Formality, distance: these were the ideas that

guided their approach to God. Anything but *Abba*. Jeremias writes
that to the Jewish mind, "it would have been disrespectful and
therefore inconceivable to address God with this familiar word."
We are no different, praying in sonorous tones, interjecting
"Thees" and "Thous" from King James English in our address.
There is little sense of "Daddy" present in style, much less in spirit.

Yet do we find Jesus' teaching liberating?

If you are like many people, the imagery of Abba is not helpful.
It is not simply that we are uncomfortable interacting with God on
this level, though most of us are; we do not have an experiential
category for such intimacy. Our earthly fathers were not men we
could talk to, particularly as if cradled in their arms. They were
stern, callous, some even abusive. Not all of us *had* an Abba, so being told God *is* one is not always helpful.

Yet rather than this becoming an impediment to the intimate
conversation God longs to have with us, perhaps it can fill our
longing hearts with all that we have dreamed of experiencing.
Imagine that wise, loving father you have always yearned for walking down a path by your side, his arm around your shoulders, listening, offering carefully chosen words of encouragement, loving
you unconditionally. Unlike your own, with this Father you don't
feel awkward, but totally at ease. You feel freedom and safety,
warmth and security. This is an image of God many must conjure
in order to explore the intimacies of prayer; letting God be the Father we never had. The great comfort is that it is not an emotional

or mental contrivance; we are simply immersing ourselves in the reality of how Jesus said to pray and to whom we are to pray.

This intimacy is, of course, about more than familial—or familiar—language. It speaks to the new nature of the prayer event itself. Voicing "Abba" as the starting point of prayer was a prelude to the tearing of the Jerusalem temple veil that separated the holy place from the most holy place. From that point forward no priest was needed to voice prayers on our behalf or to serve as mediator between us and God. Now we were able to go directly into God's presence. The writer of Hebrews speaks of this intimacy in terms of *confidence* (Hebrews 10:19). It's not simply that God is Abba, but that we are his sons and daughters, and we should pray in the fullest security of that relationship.

Prayer is drawing near to God; this cannot take place in the midst of fear. As Philip Yancey has observed, the very birth of Jesus declared the inauguration of the *approachability* of God. The God who could have roared, "who could order armies and empires about like pawns on a chessboard, this God emerged . . . as a baby who could not speak or eat solid food or control his bladder, [and] who depended on a [poor] teenage couple for shelter, food and love." God could have come to us in any way he wanted, and he chose to come as a baby. The most gentle, approachable, intimate way imaginable. God intentionally chose to relate to human beings in a manner that did not involve, or cause, fear. To encourage us to come to him confidently, boldly, as children, God came as a child himself.

And that same intent is carried through to our approach to prayer.

We need this. When the Israelites saw Mt. Sinai surrounded by thunder and lightning, trumpet blasts and smoke, they were terrified. They begged Moses to be their mediator. "Speak to us yourself and we will listen. But do not have God speak to us or we will die" (Exodus 20:19). Frederick Buechner writes that when we realize who we pray to, and the kinds of things we are asked to pray, "only the words 'Our Father' . . . make the prayer bearable."

But those two words are there.

This then is the context for prayer: the intimacy of our adoption as sons and daughters (John 1:12; Galatians 3:26). As J. B. Phillips paraphrased the apostle John's words, "Consider the incredible love that the Father has shown us in allowing us to be called 'children of God'—and that is not just what we are called, but what we *are*" (1 John 3:1 Phillips). This is not a formal, legal relationship, but a passionate, consuming, *personal* one.

We are to pray in a way that reflects the true nature of our relationship. We are children of God, and that identity should form the deepest understandings and dynamics of how we relate to him as Father. The instruction of the Lord's Prayer involved the permission to step into the fullness of our new identities in Christ. We are not to pray to God as if he is an auditor with the IRS, a highway patrol officer sitting in the speed trap or an angry parent it is best to avoid.

As a child I remember being so terrified of hell and having heard so little about God's love that I would pray—every night—for God to save me, petitioning him even though his natural bent was to despise and reject me. I had no idea of the apostle Paul's declaration in Romans: "For all who are led by the Spirit of God are children of God. So you should not be like cowering, fearful slaves. You should behave instead like God's very own children, adopted into his family—calling him 'Father, dear Father' " (Romans 8:14-15 NLT).

I am still far away from a prayer life that connects with God as Abba or fully embraces my own sonship. I've made progress over the years I've spent embracing the Christian faith, with moments of rapturous, tear-flowing intimacy, but this is too often followed by retreats into stiff, guarded dialogue produced by a dry and distant spirit. But I continue to crawl into his lap—or at least look for it—encouraged by the one truth that will not let me do otherwise: I am his child.

And Jesus knew that when he taught us how to pray, we would need to be reminded to pray like one.

Expectant

"In heaven"

I have stood in four of the most famous "squares" of the world: Red Square in Moscow, Trafalgar's Square in London, Times Square in New York, and St. Peter's Square (which is actually an oval) in Rome. Their significance was not in geography but in *meaning*. Consider St. Peter's Square; able to hold 400,000 people, it is not only the scene of large papal audiences but special commemorations, masses and beatification ceremonies. When he is in Rome, the pope makes an appearance every Sunday around 11 a.m. at the window of the Vatican Palace, addressing the crowd and blessing all present. People flock there from all over the world; not only the nearly 900 million Roman Catholics but pilgrim Protestants such as myself who understand it to be second only to Jerusalem in terms of significance to Christian history.

Place *matters*.

From the beginning of human history we have invested certain places with significance, meaning, even power. When I first visited the White House, something emanated from its halls; when I stood at Stonehenge, I could feel the thousands of lives who had revered its ground; when I gazed through the chain-link fence surrounding the remains of the World Trade Center towers only months after the attacks of September 11, I sensed the deep force of my surroundings.

But it's not just meaning; place can also bestow *significance*.

If I sign my name to an academic article from Des Moines, Iowa (nothing against those good folk), it will often mean less than if I sign from Oxford, England. Place matters, and in turn it speaks of the one who lives there. And place is brought into prayer, for we pray to the God in *heaven*.

The importance of this is often lost on us, even though the phrase "which art in heaven" can be found twenty times in the Gospel of Matthew alone. When Jesus taught us to pray to "Our Father" who is "in heaven," the admonition was not directional, as if we needed to get the right address on our prayer, but *declarative*. Jesus was leading us to reflect on the God to whom we pray.

Specifically, the God we pray to is both *immanent* and *transcendent*. These are words normally bandied around in theology classrooms, but the ideas behind these words should be in every Christian's heart.

Immanence means close by, near. God is not distant, but by our side. At first glance the idea of praying to a God in heaven might suggest the opposite, with heaven intimating that God is far off and distant. But when Jesus said that we pray to the God of "heaven," the language is actually plural. The most literal reading would be the God in the "heavens." This was a way of designating every location, every place at one time. The idea is that we do not pray to an earthbound God but one who is beyond geography, able to be with us at all times and in all places. So author and professor Dallas Willard suggests that the opening line of the Lord's Prayer might best be read, "Our Father always near us."

But the equally compelling idea, and perhaps the most suggestive, is that of God's *transcendence*. That God is not only with us but also separate from us. God comes to us from beyond this world, from outside of this world, bringing that which only he can bring. We do not pray to a God of the earth but the God of heaven. The heaven of our longing: eternal, glorified, set apart from sin and decay; the heaven of hope and glory. *This* is the abode of God, and all that it is flows from all that *he* is. We don't pray to a lifeless image, a bygone hero or a sentimental thought. We pray to the God of *heaven;* the God who is all-powerful, all-knowing and ever-present.

So we pray with *expectation* because we pray to the God who *acts*. C. S. Lewis once observed that the New Testament contains what can only be called embarrassing promises of what prayer can unleash. It's true. They border on the scandalous. "I tell you the truth, if you have faith and do not doubt, . . . you can say to this mountain, 'Go, throw yourself into the sea,' and it will be done. If you believe, you will receive whatever you ask for in prayer," Jesus maintained (Matthew 21:21-22).

But as J. B. Phillips once argued, most do not pray to this God. Instead of a father in heaven, the God we pray to is a father on earth. Along with having a parent who can dishearten us toward the idea of God as Abba (the relational side of things), we can also assess God's abilities in light of the limitation of what our earthly father was able to do. J. B. Phillips calls this having a parental hang-over, raising the provocative question, "Is your God too small?"

Several years ago my oldest daughter and I were driving to the grocery store. Only five at the time, Rebecca asked me where the sun came from. I told her that God made the sun. I told her that God made everything—including her—and that God loved her very much. She then asked, "Daddy, what does God look like?" I said, "I don't know, honey. What do you think he looks like?" She didn't even pause. She said, "I think he looks just like you." Consciously or not, we all once felt this way about our earthly fathers. The dilemma is that many of us still do. Once again, if we had a good and strong father, this works positively. If not, it can be a life-long struggle. The God we pray to becomes filled with all of the weaknesses, inadequacies and shortcomings of our parent.

And that is a very small God.

But it is not the God we pray to. We pray to the transcendent God, the God of heaven, the God who can act. And act in ways that only God can. Which means supernaturally.

Many of us who follow Christ have an odd relationship with the supernatural. We believe in it but never expect to experience it. Truth be told, it would be more than a bit unsettling to us if we did. When we pray to God, we believe he can do whatever he wants; we just don't expect him to act in ways that are, well, Godlike. The prayers for miraculous intervention are prayed perfunctorily, but not passionately or expectantly.

If you want to be jolted into remembering just what God can do, travel to Rome. Everywhere you turn there are shrines and churches built in the memory of God performing one supernatural act or another. It almost becomes numbing after a while, yet leaving you with a deep sense that Christians pray to a God who can do whatever he jolly well pleases, regardless of how it might fit into the normal ordering of things. This came home to me while I was in the ancient section of the city, where I visited a subterranean prison that supposedly once housed the apostle Peter. Legend has it that he converted the jailer, and a spring that still flows today miraculously came into existence for the new convert's baptism. The site was far from the most spectacular of holy places, and certainly had less drama than others. Yet I found myself alone, dipping my fingers into the well, wondering of its true origin.

Was I kneeling by a miracle? And what would that mean if I was?

The answer is found in what is also throughout Rome: people praying.

Not, as it might be caricatured, praying to the shrines themselves but praying by the shrine as a reminder of the power and ability of the God to whom they prayed.

I recently prayed for a woman on our church staff in her second trimester of pregnancy. She and her husband had just discovered their unborn daughter had a brain stem, but no brain. They made the decision to carry the child full-term, wanting to give God any and every opportunity to perform a miracle. While their faith did not demand this of God, their faith could not deny God the opportunity. Twenty or more of our staff gathered. I anointed her with oil; we all reached out and placed our hands on her—many of the women on our staff laying their hands on her stomach.

On their behalf and as their pastor representing the people of God, I prayed.

I do not remember what I said, but I recall a single realization that flashed through my mind. "God could really do this. He could give this child a brain." Suddenly this wasn't simply an act of obedience; it was an act of expectancy.

We were, after all, praying to a God in heaven.

Several weeks later I held the horribly deformed child in my arms in the hospital room, and a few days later, stood with the parents by the tiny grave in which their little girl was buried. Did this diminish the expectancy I now bring to prayer? Did it for the young couple who held out hope to the bitter end? No. In the midst of the sadness, a deep realization was forged that the season of prayer offered for her life was decisive.

The importance of praying in the realization that we pray to the God in heaven is not related to whether or not he responds in the way we would most desire; the importance of praying to the God *in heaven* is related to the faith that this is a God who can and does act. And that is the point. We prayed because God *could* have healed her. He *could* have miraculously intervened. Such prayer does not simply invite him to do whatever he might will, but it places all of life within the context of his governing care. Failing to pursue this most elemental reflection of faith would be to fail to acknowledge that there is, indeed, a God in heaven.

Many of us have incredible burdens, problems that are overwhelming us, pressures that seem beyond our ability to survive. Yet we don't ask God for help. Somehow we don't truly believe that God has the power to do anything about it. In truth, God can do anything, and he's just waiting for us to recognize his power and *ask*.

The God in heaven is the God who has power over nature. He is the God who has power over circumstances and events. He is the God who has power over individual lives.

Paul challenges the vision of our thinking when he writes, "[God] is able to do immeasurably more than all we ask or imagine, according to his power that is at work within us" (Ephesians 3:20). The key word for many of us is *imagine*. What can you imagine? Bill Hybels has written about being too busy *not* to pray. He is right. If I'm too busy to pray, then I'm too busy to have the power I need to see my life affected by God. When we work at life, that's all there is—*our* work, but when we pray, *God* works. James writes that, "The prayer of a person living right with God is something powerful" (James 5:16 *The Message*).

So what *can* we pray for? Is anything off limits? Actually, no. I'm assuming we're omitting prayers that are obviously base and evil, such as prayers for someone to be abused or maligned. (Though I have been sorely tempted from time to time to pray for God to dole out a good smiting or two.) What tempts and often confuses us is our struggle with the "health and wealth" matters. Many Christians have appropriately dismissed the "name it, claim it" theology that treats God as little more than a cosmic errand boy who, through prayer, serves our pursuit of affluence. Yet in so doing, we have forgotten about the freedom we have to come before God in prayer for anything we want. Yes, the house with the backyard, the job, the healing, the husband or wife, the child. How could we keep such things away from the kind of community God is after in prayer? It may not be in God's perfect will for our lives, but it is not wrong to lay all of our life and its desires before God. We must never forget that we pray to Abba, who longs to give us the desires of our heart. We'll get to praying for his kingdom and will in a moment, which, of course, informs much of this, but first things first.

When you pray, you pray to a God in heaven. Jesus said to pray like you know it.

———————&———————

Reverent

"Hallowed be your name."

I was born with the given name of James Emery White. My grandfather's name was Henry James White, and my great-grandfather's name was Robert Emery Thompson. So the names "James" and "Emery" were part of my heritage. Today, friends call me Jim. But that was not what I was called at birth. I was called *Emery*. And not just at birth but on every day, by every single person in my life, for the first five years of my life. That was my name: *Emery* White. From birth, my parents chose to call me by my middle name. It was the only name I went by and the only name that entered my parent's mind when they thought of their son.

On the first day of kindergarten, when everybody was learning everybody else's name, one of the children made a mistake with mine. Instead of calling me Emery, she called me "Ann Marie." Close, but not the same. I was none too pleased. Hell hath no fury like that of a five-year-old who has his name mispronounced on the first day of kindergarten, much less when that five-year-old is a boy, and the mispronunciation gives him the name of a *girl!* Even at five, I knew what was at stake. I came home, gathered my family around me, and said, "I have decided that I am not going to be called Emery anymore. I want to be called Jim. That is what I want my name to be." You can imagine how that went over with my parents, who had *chosen* the name and had *called* me Emery for five years. My parents were not quite sure how to respond; they decided to see how long it would last.

I have been Jim ever since.

How our names are treated matter to us. It matters to God too. In the third of the ten commandments, God declares, "You shall not misuse the name of the LORD your God, for the LORD will not hold anyone guiltless who misuses his name" (Exodus 20:7). Why? Because God's name represents God himself, his very nature and being. So Jesus teaches us that when we pray, God's name is to be "hallowed," which means honored. To give honor to the name of God through prayer means that it is *revered.* Reverence toward God in prayer balances the intimacy we have through our identity as sons and daughters of God. As Andrew Murray notes, it takes the central word of the Old Testament, *holy,* and joins it with the central word of the New Testament, *Father.* We pray *Abba,* but with the honor and respect due his Being. As Augustine wrote, "[it is] not as if the name of God were not holy already, but that it may be held holy by men; i.e., that God may so become known to them, that they shall reckon nothing more holy, and which they are more afraid of offending."

Will Willimon and Stanley Hauerwas write of a college student who became the first person in his family to go to college. Someone approached the student and offered him some illegal drugs, saying, "Go ahead, try it. It'll make you feel good."

"No," the student replied.

"Don't be so uptight," said the drug dealer. "Nobody is going to know that you tried a little dope, got a little high."

"That's not the point," said the student. "The point is that my mother cleaned houses and washed floors to send me to this college. I am here because of her. I am here for her. I wouldn't do anything that might demean her sacrifice for me."

That is honoring a name.

This was understood by the Jewish people. Prior to the great exodus from Egypt, they knew that Moses stumbled upon the burning bush. Through that epiphany, God himself spoke to Moses, telling him to go to Pharaoh to demand that he release all of his Hebrew slaves. Moses asked God to give him his name—the very name of God—so that he could say to the people exactly who had sent him. The answer God gave to Moses was intriguing: "God said to Moses, 'I AM WHO I AM. This is what you are to say: . . . "I AM has sent me to you"'" (Exodus 3:14). "I AM" came to be considered the most holy word in existence to the Jewish people, for it was the very name of God. It was so revered that the Jews would not even pronounce it, and later would not add vowel points, resulting in YHWH.[†]

So how do we honor God's name in prayer? It is tempting to reduce reverence to form and style, and there is certainly a place for reverence to be introduced in this manner. Consider the great medieval cathedrals, designed to create awe and inspire worship. Reverence is brought to bear on the human spirit by simply entering. Before the day of the cathedral, much of the design of the Jerusalem temple was to emphasize the honor due God by those who came to pray. As physical beings moved by our senses and shaped by our context, there is a place for such things.

But the temptation is to make such things the heart of what it means to hallow the name of God as opposed to that which *supports* the hallowing of the name of God. To pray in a way that reveres the name of God is to pray that every day our *lives* will become more holy in devotion to God. As the third-century bishop Cyprian of Carthage wrote, God is not made more holy by our prayer; rather, we pray that his holy name may daily be made holy in us.

God's name has to do with God's *reputation*. We honor his name to the degree that we enhance his reputation.

Barnabas is an easily overlooked character in the New Testament. He doesn't appear until the fourth chapter of the book of Acts, but he makes quite an entrance:

[†] Early on, the missing vowels were mistakenly assumed to create the word "Jehovah." Closer to the actual name would be "Yahweh."

All the believers were one in heart and mind. No one claimed that any of his possessions was his own, but they shared everything they had. With great power the apostles continued to testify to the resurrection of the Lord Jesus, and much grace was upon them all. . . .

Joseph, a Levite from Cyprus, whom the apostles called Barnabas (which means Son of Encouragement), sold a field he owned and brought the money and put it at the apostles' feet. (Acts 4:32-33, 36)

It was a time of great expectation and enthusiasm—God was working, people were responding to the message, there was great growth. It was also a time of great anxiety and great need. How would they make it? How would they survive? Would this enterprise, called the church, that Jesus came to establish even get off the ground? Enter Barnabas, establishing a tone for the entire community by selflessly selling some land and giving the money to fund what the church was trying to do and be.

Just a few chapters later, in Acts 9, we find a man by the name of Saul, who had persecuted the church as an official representative of the leaders who had crucified Jesus. His goal had been the persecution, arrest, imprisonment and even murder of Christians. When Luke, the author of Acts, searched for a word to describe Saul's torrent of destructive rage, he seized on a Greek term that spoke of a beast tearing apart flesh with its jaws (Acts 8:3). Saul was a nasty man with a nasty reputation; he was greatly feared by all of the followers of Jesus.

Saul became a follower of Christ. It was real, sincere, genuine and authentic, but nobody believed it. They thought he was faking it in order to infiltrate the church to find out where Christians met, how many there were and the identities of the main leaders. Again, enter Barnabas:

> [Saul] tried to join the disciples, but they were all afraid of him. They didn't trust him one bit. Then Barnabas took him under his wing. He introduced him to the apostles and stood up for him. . . .
>
> After that he was accepted as one of them, . . . no questions asked. (Acts 9:26-28 *The Message*)

Barnabas threw his weight and reputation and credibility behind Saul in order to get him accepted by the leaders of the church. He risked everything for someone else. It was a totally selfless act. One that had nothing but the well-being, the advancement, of another in mind. And what did it produce? The man who would later be known as the apostle Paul became one of the most influential figures in all of Christian history. He wrote the bulk of what we now refer to as the New Testament, and he single-handedly extended the church throughout the world, going on mission after mission in order to plant churches where the name of Christ had never even been heard.

Moving ahead with Barnabas, in Acts 11 we find that the news of Christ and his resurrection from the dead was spreading. People were becoming followers of Christ in bewildering numbers, even in places where there was no church. One of those places was Antioch:

> When the church in Jerusalem got wind of this, they sent Barnabas to Antioch to check on things. As soon as he arrived, he saw that God was behind and in it all. He threw himself in with them, got behind them, urging them to stay with it the rest of their lives. He was a good man that way, enthusiastic and confident in the Holy Spirit's ways. The community grew large and strong. . . .
>
> [He was] there a whole year, meeting with the church and teaching a lot of people. It was in Antioch that the disciples were for the first time called Christians. (Acts 11:22-24, 26 *The Message*)

For me, this is the crowning moment in the life of Barnabas. It wasn't the investment of a year but the legacy of a life. The word *Christians* means "little Christs." This is the goal of prayer. To earn the title "Christian" in the most direct sense of its meaning—to so live for Christ that we are linked with his name, not in derision but in honor.

Unfortunately, this is not the honor that all Christ followers bring. As German philosopher Friedrich Nietzsche once challenged, "Show me that you are redeemed and then I will believe in your redeemer." We cannot feign to be one person in prayer while being another once off of our knees. Our prayer *and* our lives must honor the name of the One to whom we pray.

Evelyn Underhill suggests turning to the Old Testament story of Araunah the Jebusite for insight into the deepest dynamic of honor.

King David is directed to build an altar to God on Araunah's threshing floor. This was no small matter. Araunah's threshing floor was the basis for his entire subsistence.

First an angel came to Araunah, then King David himself. David asks for the threshing floor and offers a fair price. Araunah is not content to give what is asked. Overwhelmed with the obvious importance of the request, not to mention the intended purpose of the floor, he refuses all monies and gives it freely. He then offers the oxen for the burned offerings, the threshing sledges for the wood and the wheat for the grain offering. "I will give all this," he declares (1 Chronicles 21:23).

Underhill notes that in a single moment a man had an opportunity to honor God with the totality of his life; with his work, his achievements, his future needs, the very tools of his craft and food for the coming winter. In so doing, the site for generations of prayers was not simply *declared* holy but *made* holy.

> Thus the site of Solomon's Temple was sanctified; and a place was prepared for the Holy of Holies, the Ark and the Mercy

Seat. Those who stand today in the temple area of Jerusalem, stand on the threshing floor which was offered without condition by [Araunah] the Jebusite. There Isaiah saw the Seraphim; there the child Jesus, near the end of its long history, was presented before God; there he watched the widow give her mite; then he cast out those who dared to mingle man's profit with God's praise. An unbroken chain leads from the farmer's offering to the Cross.

And so we too pray:

Our father, who art in heaven, hallowed be thy name.

Submitted

"Your kingdom come, your will be done
on earth as it is in heaven."

At the 1948 Urbana Student Mission Convention, plenary speaker Norton Sterrett asked, "How many of you who are concerned about the will of God spend five minutes a day asking him to show you his will?" A young man by the name of Paul Little was sitting in the audience, and he later reflected that it was as if somebody had grabbed him by the throat:

> At that time I was an undergraduate, concerned about what I should do when I graduated from the university. I was running around campus—going to this meeting, reading that book, trying to find somebody's little formula—1, 2, 3, 4 and a bell rings—and I was frustrated out of my mind trying to figure out the will of God. I was doing everything but getting into the presence of God and asking him to show it to me.

Immediately after addressing God as our Abba who acts and with a reminder that as his children we are to care for and honor his name, we are to seek his will for our lives.

Emphasis on the *his*.

Which means we pray in a way that searches out what God wants, what God cares about and what matters most to God.

It means to pray in order to find out what God is doing, and then willingly join with him to do it.

It means to pray in such a way as to bring our life into alignment with his agenda.

We think, wrote Søren Kierkegaard, when we pray that the important thing is that God hears what we pray for.

> And yet in the true, eternal sense it is just the reverse: the true relation in prayer is not when God hears what is prayed for, but when *the person praying* continues to pray until he is *the one who hears,* who hears what God wills. Our natural bent is to use many words to make demands in our prayer; "the true man of prayer," observed Kierkegaard, "only *attends.*"

Why is this the most spiritually significant aspect of prayer? Because the heart of our sin, the genesis of our broken relationship with God, is pride—the antithesis to seeking and submitting to God's will. Satan's downfall, and ours as well, was the desire to be gods ourselves and have our will contend with God's. To pray for

God's kingdom begins with placing it above our own. And make no mistake, this elevation of God's will over ours is what it means to lead a spiritual life. Teresa of Ávila aptly noted that even the beginner in prayer should first "labour and be resolute and prepare [themselves] with all possible diligence to bring [their] will into conformity with the will of God."

Nothing else holds primacy.

Every day a battle rages within human souls between the will of God and the human will. When we approach God in prayer, the battle does not cease; in some ways, it intensifies because then all is on the line. Will we pray for our will or *his?* Will the prayer be an effort to convince God to grant my desires, or for him to plant *his* desires in me? When I ask for *his* guidance, will I listen? Do I even *desire* to? As Origen once counseled, people who truly pray for the coming of the kingdom of God are actually praying that the kingdom of God be established in their lives.

We should not be casual about this or underestimate the arduous nature of the task. It is one thing to acknowledge a king; it's quite another to allow your self to be ruled.

I find this aspect of prayer theologically decisive and personally overwhelming. I know that I don't want to be outside of God's will. I know that God's kingdom effort is paramount, and there is no life outside of its gates, no matter the temptation. But placing myself in the flow of his will, asking only for his kingdom to be built, and not mine, shakes me to the core of my being. This is because I am self-centered and self-absorbed, and I do not want to give up my own desires for his. There is something, somewhere deep inside, that questions God's character.

Somewhere I recall reading how astounding it was for so many people to affirm the unquenchable love of God, yet be so terribly afraid of his will. It is as if we think following God's will must somehow bring wounding—not just the short term wounds of radical obedience but ultimate wounds in terms of life's final prize. Thus as we pray for God's will the hidden agenda is that our capacity to trust in his answer would be expanded. Kierkegaard was right in defining prayer as "a silent surrendering of everything to God."

So when I pray the Lord's Prayer, it is part of a larger, ongoing journey of relationship, intimacy, love, sacrifice and submission—and in the end, death.

Death is a process few of us think about, much less understand. We refuse to, for it is the one topic we do not want to consider. In 1969 Elisabeth Kübler-Ross published her groundbreaking book *On Death and Dying*. Drawing from years of research, most while at the University of Chicago, she concluded that those who are confronted with a terminal illness go through five stages on their journey toward death: denial, anger, bargaining, depression and finally acceptance. Far from a neat, chronological progression, we dart from one to another, going backward and forward. Yet together these are the dynamics when it comes to the death of our bodies.

It is no different when it comes to the death of *self*. Or at least when that is what the will of God is calling us to pursue.

First comes denial. We cannot bring ourselves to admit that this is what God would have us do, much less experience. The loss of our *own* will, our *own* dreams, is too great to consider. It seems suicidal. Which, of course, it is.

Then comes anger as we project the pain of the loss onto those around us—including God. Have you ever noticed the number of fist-shaking tirades hurled toward God from those in the Bible who were on their way to becoming saints? From David's "How long?" to Jeremiah's "You have seduced me!"

Next we bargain with God, attempting to earn something that is more to our liking. From the blatant "God, I promise I will go to church, give up smoking and start tithing" to the more subtle "Father, this is what I could do for you and what it would mean if events could go this way. It really is how I could best honor and serve."

As we face the unmistakable call to die to ourselves, we can experience depression. Why depression? Because in submission to God's will we see death, not life.

Then, in the end comes acceptance.

But here is where the analogy to physical death breaks down, because from a spiritual perspective *acceptance* is not where the journey ends. There is a sixth step, one that moves from acceptance to worship. It is coming to see the will of God for what it truly is: *heaven*.

Many do not complete their pilgrimage of prayer, often languishing in the bitterness of depression. Or more likely at the first stage of denial, exercising our will to chart the course of our own destiny. Which, if left unchecked, also has a series of steps, a downward spiral into a dark abyss ending not in heaven but hell. As C. S. Lewis notes, we can either say in this life, "Thy will be done," or hear God say at the end of our life, "*Thy* will be done."

So while "Thy will be done" is submission, it must not be mere submission. C. S. Lewis writes that if we make progress in this area, "Thy will be done" will move from submission to the declaration of joyful desire. To make it submission alone would "greatly impoverish the prayer." That is the intent of the prayer itself: to pray "Thy will be done" with resolve and adoration.

Such was the model of the often overlooked Habakkuk.

Standing alone among the prophets, Habakkuk did not bring the word of God to the people; Habakkuk brought the people's words to God during a time of great upheaval and unrest, full of violence and political change. Habakkuk's lifetime saw Judah invaded and Jerusalem destroyed by the Babylonians. Adding insult to injury, it was also a time of rampant immorality. Habakkuk did not hesitate to bring his will and the apparent course of God into confrontation through prayer—beginning with both anger and denial. Anger that God had not acted: "How long, O LORD, must I call for help, / but you do not listen?" (Habakkuk 1:2), and denial that this was actually what God had in mind:

Why do you make me look at injustice?
Why do you tolerate wrong? . . .
Therefore the law is paralyzed,
and justice never prevails.
The wicked hem in the righteous,
so that justice is perverted. (Habakkuk 1:3-4)

God responded in a way Habakkuk would have never envisioned. In essence God said, "You're right. Things are a mess. And I'm going to deal with it. I'm going to empower your worst enemy—the Babylonians—and then I'm going to turn them loose to ravage your land and bring judgment."

This is not what Habakkuk had in mind.

What Habakkuk wanted was for God to intervene graciously and send revival, for evil leaders to be judged, a new kingdom set up in the land, the nation itself to escape judgment and the people spared. Instead, God declared that he was going to send in the infidels and destroy everything. God had warned the people time and again, and they had proven they would not listen. Prophet after prophet, calamity after calamity, the people had hardened their hearts. God's longsuffering had ended. He was now going to act.

So much for anger.

Then came Habakkuk's bargaining stage. He prays again, asking how a holy God could use a wicked nation to punish his own people. Yes, the people of Judah deserved judgment, but the Babylonians were worse! If he was going to dish out judgment, shouldn't it start there? "Your eyes are too pure to look on evil; / you cannot tolerate wrong," Habakkuk answered (Habakkuk 1:13).

In one of the most fascinating dialogues recorded in Scripture, God responded to Habakkuk, acknowledging the evil of the Babylonians and that indeed judgment *will* come their way. Yet his plan would remain the same, and Judah should wait patiently while God's justice makes its way through time and place.

This does not make Habakkuk happy.

Fully confronted with God's will, there is clear depression. And it is voiced to God every bit as much as his anger. "You have made men like fish in the sea . . . / The wicked foe pulls all of them up with hooks" (Habakkuk 1:14-15). What good is having you as my God when this is how life turns out? This is the crucible of faith—is life best with God, or without God? Few have journeyed long in relationship with God apart from this defining moment. "What good are you, God, if my life is filled with sadness, terror, trauma and pain? Let me pursue my will; at least I will pursue my own best interests."

Habakkuk lingers there for a moment, but little more. He senses something deeper pulling him in to more eternal realities. Habakkuk chooses to journey to the place of acceptance.

And not just acceptance, but worship.

A prayer of Habakkuk the prophet. . . .
LORD, I have heard of your fame;

> I stand in awe of your deeds, O LORD.
> Renew them in our day,
> > in our time make them known; . . .
> [Y]et I will rejoice in the LORD,
> > I will be joyful in God my Savior.
> The Sovereign LORD is my strength;
> > he makes my feet like the feet of a deer,
> > he enables me to go on the heights.
> > (Habakkuk 3:1-2, 18-19)

Habakkuk prayed, "God, be God."

Reflect on that for a moment.

"God, *be* God . . ." in my life, in my thinking, in my will. Be the One, eternal, all-knowing Being who loves me more than I love myself. Your will is nothing but you in my life. So God, *be God.*

The rigorous faith needed for this is staggering. To pray it apart from all the courage you can muster would be to fail to understand what you are praying. Particularly concerning God's utter and complete sovereignty. For God's will to be done, his kingdom to come—what would that mean? "What would stand and what would fall?" reflects Frederick Buechner. "Who would be welcomed in and who be thrown the Hell out? . . . Boldness indeed. To speak those words is to invite the tiger out of the cage, to unleash a power that makes atomic power look like a warm breeze."

But this is not just a private, personal, individual affair.

When we pray, we are to pray for God's kingdom, God's *will*, not only to come into our lives and take root, but through us to spread throughout the earth. God's kingdom was announced by Jesus, and makes its way into the world from that beachhead as individuals give their hearts and lives to Christ. In that sense God's kingdom has arrived, and we have been brought into that kingdom as believers. But the full consummation lies ahead. So to pray that the kingdom will come is to pray that his kingdom will grow as we pursue our witness to Jesus and live lives of salt and light. So with the Great Commission comes a *cultural* commission. We pray for the kingdom to take hold on the planet, in governments and institutions, judicial systems and media.

I was in Johannesburg, South Africa, on the tenth anniversary of the end of apartheid. That day was borne on the prayer for God's kingdom to come.

Years before I was in Moscow, worshiping in a church filled to capacity. Seeing the front rows filled with women wearing scarves, singing with a passion and intensity that was captivating, I leaned over to the pastor and asked through my interpreter who the women were. He answered, "Those are the women who prayed communism out of Russia."

The kingdom is meant to *come*.

"The real Christian," writes Evelyn Underhill, "is always a revolutionary." Or as John Stott writes, "What Jesus bids us pray is that life on earth may come to approximate more nearly to life in heaven." Just as this is *prayed* by individuals, the inescapable fact is that God's kingdom on earth is to *begin* with us as individuals. We pray for God's will to be done on earth, and then we rise from our knees to meet the challenge. Indeed, the time of prayer is what binds us to action in the first place.

In fourteenth-century England there were holy women who placed themselves in little rooms at the base of churches and gave themselves to prayer. They prayed for the church and its members and the extension of the kingdom of God. These women were called by the quaint but telling name of "anchoress," for they were spiritual anchors that held the church amid the storms of that century. This is why prayer must never fall into a passivity of spirit. Instead it is a frontal assault on the evil one and the farcical "kingdom" he is attempting to establish in rebellion against the true kingdom of God. Evelyn Underhill noted:

> To say day by day "Thy Kingdom Come"—if these tremendous words really stand for a conviction and desire—does not mean "I quite hope that some day the Kingdom of God will be established, and peace and goodwill prevail. But at present I don't see how it is to be managed or what I can do about it." On the contrary, it means, or should mean, "Here am I! Send me!"—active, costly collaboration with the Spirit in who we believe.

As Tennyson wrote, "More things are wrought by prayer than this world dreams of." Or more to the point, more things are meant to be wrought by prayer than any of us allow ourselves to dream.

But there is yet a final layer we must pull back.

Praying along these lines is when our eternal role is being shaped. God is in the soul-making business; but not just for our time on earth. He's shaping us for eternity. We have a rather full future ahead of us. In talking about that future, the Bible speaks of becoming joint heirs with Christ and glorified with Christ (Romans 8:17), and reigning with Christ (2 Timothy 2:12; Revelation 20:6). Even judging the angels (1 Corinthians 6:3).

Without reading too much into the varying crowns we will receive and other eschatological material that fills far too many books with little more than speculation, I am personally convinced that we will have specific roles and responsibilities throughout eternity in direct proportion to our faithfulness and submission here on earth. The parable of the talents, set in an eschatological context, suggests as much.

At the very least, heaven will not be a static community but a dynamic one, filled with activity and purpose, meaning and significance, service and leadership. We will have jobs and tasks, adventures and missions. As a result much of the call to prayer is for our training and development. As we form ourselves according to his will, it is as if we are carving out our role in the kingdom to come. As we pray over the growing kingdom of God on earth and the coming completion of the kingdom, we prepare ourselves to govern it, for we are active participants with God in bringing it to reality. Our prayers cultivate our role in God's ongoing work throughout eternity.

So this prayer both influences eternity and creates our role within it. Those most in line with God's will here and now will have the most stake in it in the world to come.

That's part of praying for the kingdom to come.

And the more we are part of it now, the more we are preparing ourselves for our part in it then.

Interlude

$\mathcal{N}$ow we must take an important pause. Not long, but an important moment nonetheless.

It is has not escaped even the most casual of observers that the Lord's Prayer presents itself in two movements. First it ascends to the heights of heaven, and then it returns to the plains of earth. It directs us vertically, then horizontally; first we focus on God, then on us; there is attention to the One prayed *to* and then to the one who is praying. Tertullian linked this to Jesus' admonition to first seek the kingdom of God and then all other things will be added to you.

Our prayers begin with a look to God's name, God's kingdom, God's will; then we move toward *our* needs—daily sustenance, forgiveness, deliverance.

There is more at hand here than prayer beginning with the primacy of God before it moves to the petty concerns of human life. When we begin our prayers with a look to the person and character of God, coupled with his agenda for the world, it dramatically informs as to *how* we pray for our needs, *how* we look at our sin and *how* we need his presence. Without first praying in a way that reflects intimacy, reverence and submission, I doubt I would pray in the spirit of dependency, humility and honesty.

So the order matters.

But it is also a reminder of the greatness of God's love and concern for us. This God of heaven—the One whose name is to be honored, whose kingdom will come—*cares!* Yet this also raises the deepest of struggles, that of unanswered prayer. So after examining the invitation to pray for our daily needs, our daily forgiveness and our daily deliverance, we will turn our attention to those moments when we feel that God is anything but part of the day for which we prayed.

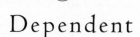

FIVE

Dependent

"Give us today our daily bread."

$\mathcal{D}$uring a trip to Lusaka, Zambia, I met with a young AIDS orphan. She does not have the disease but has been left parentless through its destructive force. The AIDS pandemic has virtually wiped out an entire generation in Africa, leaving the very young and the very old in its wake.

Susanne is in the sixth grade and lives with a distant relative. Her home is a thatched hut; in order to drink she has to walk what we would consider a great distance to draw water from a hole in the ground surrounded by animal feces. She eats corn for almost every meal; it is all their subsistence farming can produce. The clothes she wears today are likely the ones she wore the day before and will wear tomorrow.

We talked through an interpreter about the education she was now receiving, her favorite game (a form of basketball called "net" ball) and a bit about where she was living.

When it came time to leave, I told her that I would be praying for her, and she startled me by immediately replying that she would be praying for *me*. As I drove away through the bush, leaving the village where we had met, I thought about how different our prayers would be.

I would pray for her daily bread. Literally.

I would pray that she would have sanitary drinking water; that she wouldn't be raped by some man thinking (as many in Zambia do) that sex with a virgin would rid him of the HIV virus. I would pray that she could continue to stay with the family that was raising her, and that she could continue to attend the small school.

And what would she pray for me? Undoubtedly, the same thing. She knows nothing else.

She will pray that I have food to eat, water to drink, health to enjoy; that I will have a bed to lie in and be protected from assault.

The easiest prayer to pray is the emergency prayer, the one that calls out for immediate rescue. It is also the most natural (even those who are not in relationship with God will call on his name in crisis). The *hardest* prayer is often its opposite: the prayer for mundane, everyday needs. Prayers that are important, but not urgent: this is the meaning of the word Jesus used when instructing us to pray for our daily bread—*epiousios*—literally the "bread for tomorrow." Jesus spoke these words in a culture in which laborers were usually hired on a daily basis, and basic foods such as bread could not be preserved. The daily dependence for life's most foundational needs was keenly felt. More than we do today, they understood that getting their daily bread was a matter of prayer.

Which is why today, the blandest line in the Lord's Prayer may very well be for our daily needs. The greatest miracles, the most incredible blessings, were often tied to daily provision; now they are taken for granted. They only become items of prayer when taken away; then we realize that no other prayer is of greater import. In setting this dynamic of prayer into motion, Jesus wanted us to avoid presumption and maintain a healthy sense of our dependency at all times. Not merely as an emotional repositioning but as a reality; in truth, I *don't* have what it takes to survive this day, and God knows it. I need to pray for the most basic needs of my life because I cannot generate them on my own. Yes, I am called to work in whatever way possible to provide for myself and my family; I am to be responsible with what I have been given so that I do not squander that which is brought my way.

As William Barclay once wrote, "If we prayed this petition and then simply sat down with folded hands and waited, we would quite certainly starve." Yet all of our efforts must be seen as means for his provision, while never assuming that we are ever truly self-sufficient.

And this is hard. Let's be candid; we do not want to be dependent on anyone or anything, yet the prayer God wants calls for a daily declaration of this very thing. When the apostle Paul wrote to the church in Philippi: "Do not be anxious about anything, but in everything, by prayer and petition, with thanksgiving, present your requests to God" (Philippians 4:6), it was not simply for encouragement. It was a *command*.

But there is more to this aspect of prayer than mere dependence. It reveals the nature of our relationship with God, one that harkens back to his place as Abba. Praying for daily bread could seem too material to bring before God or too trivial to bother him with. Yet Richard Foster suggests that the life of Jesus was meant to demonstrate God's occupation with what might be seen as the trivialities of life. He provided wine for those who were celebrating, food for those who were hungry, rest for those who were weary. He went out of his way to find the "little people": the poor, the sick, the powerless. "So it is fully in order," concludes Foster, "that he invites us to pray for daily bread."

So we come to God and say:

- Give me today the insight and patience I need to raise my children.

- Give me today the sensitivity and commitment I need for my marriage.

- Give me today the money I need, the job that I need, the knowledge I need, the strength I need.

Not in a spirit that *demands* but in a spirit that *depends*.

And it is to be a *daily* dependence. There is a phrase which says, "God is seldom early, but never late." Beyond this just-in-time delivery system, God also commonly seems to refrain from excess.

Throughout the forty years of wilderness wandering, the manna came—but only for that day's needs. The people wanted to hoard, to hedge, to set aside, yet God supernaturally designed the provision to be sufficient for that day, but not beyond. They would have to depend on God for their daily bread *daily*.

Yet the intent runs even deeper. To pray for our daily bread goes beyond a sense of dependence; it reminds us that our prayers should not go much *beyond* our daily needs. The Bible says: "When you ask, you do not receive, because you ask with wrong motives, that you may spend what you get on your pleasures" (James 4:3). If our prayers are along the lines of "Make me famous, make me rich and throw in the best parking spaces," we have left the sense of "daily bread" that should mold our prayers.

At first, James's injunction might seem to go against the earlier suggestion that we have the freedom to come before God in prayer for anything we want (chapter 2). However, the Greek word for "spend" is *dapanao,* and carries with it a negative connotation along the lines of its use in the parable of the prodigal son (Luke 15:13-14). James's concern is asking with wrong motives and self-ish pleasures at odds with the cause of Christ. Wrong motives lead to praying for wrong things. Such prayer assumes a level of conceit in that the one praying assumes to know what is best for his or her life. This is far different from the freedom we have to lay our heart's desires before God in submission to his heavenly power and will.

But what of those who do not have such bread? Do not millions

of such people pray this very prayer? Famine and starvation are realities in our world; water, basic shelter and adequate clothing escape much of the world's population.

Far from an indictment of God, this brings an indictment on us.
Praying for my daily bread carries with it the idea that perhaps as
I pray I may be the means to provide God's bread to another who
is praying. In fact, that may be the point.

Now some would want to add a final layer of meaning to these
words, namely, praying for the daily, heavenly bread of the Eucharist, or Lord's Supper. Protestants are often mystified by the role the
Eucharist plays in the spiritual life of our Catholic brothers and sis-
ters. Some of this is theological; some of it is how Protestants have
reduced communion to little more than saltine crackers and grape
juice that leaves our throats out of sorts for the next hymn.

It's more. Far more.

Henri Nouwen once wrote how the husband of a friend of his, a
man by the name of Bob, died suddenly of a heart attack. His friend
decided to keep her two young children away from the funeral. She
thought it would be too hard for them to see their father put in the
ground. And so for years after Bob's death the cemetery remained a
fearful and a dangerous place for them. Then, one day, the mother
asked Henri to visit the grave with her, and she invited her children
to come along. The oldest one was too afraid to go, but the younger
one decided to come with them. When they came to the place
where Bob was buried, the three of them sat down on the grass

around the headstone that was engraved with the words "A kind and gentle man." And as they sat, they reminisced about Bob.

Suddenly Nouwen said:

"Maybe one day we should have a picnic here. This is not only a place to think about death, but also a place to rejoice in our life. I think Bob will be most honored when we find new strength, here, to live." At first it seemed a strange idea: having a meal on top of a tombstone. A meal to bring strength for living. But as he said it, he realized it wasn't a strange idea at all, nor was it that original. That was exactly what Jesus asked his followers to do in remembrance of him. To have a meal of bread and wine in remembrance of his death. And from that meal, to draw strength to live. A few days later his friend took her oldest child to the grave, the younger one having convinced his sister that there was nothing to fear. Now they often go to the cemetery and tell each other stories about Bob.

Regardless of one's theology, the Lord's Supper is never *mere* symbol. It must remain for all the central act and high point of Christian worship. Yet as much as Protestants often miss the importance of the Lord's Supper for regular, spiritual sustenance, I am unconvinced that Jesus intended us to interpret this part of the prayer as a reminder to pray for the ability to partake of the Supper on a regular basis. I do not mean to suggest that the prayer is simply for physical needs; we should all pray for our daily, heavenly bread. Yet to root this solely in the Eucharist fails to encompass the wide use of bread as a spiritual metaphor throughout the New Testament.

If taken beyond the meaning of the physical necessities of life, which I think it can be, it should be expanded to include all of the spiritual necessities of life intimated in our dependence on Jesus as the bread of life. Behind the idea of Jesus revealing himself as the "bread of life" was the ancient and widespread desire for a food that would impart everlasting life. Understandably, the disciples said, "give us this bread" (John 6:34). Jesus' answer? I am what you are asking for. Those who wish to continually partake in that eternal life must know that it is Jesus himself who is the bread, and he will give it to those who come to him. This stands against there being such bread from any other quarter. Yet this feast is far from limited to the Eucharist.

So we pray for our daily bread and offer that prayer in every sense of the word.

But why?

Why pray for our daily needs and spiritual sustenance, when God already knows that we have those needs? This is one of the more common and persistent questions raised concerning prayer. John Wesley is famed for saying, "God will do nothing on earth except in answer to believing prayer." But why?

The answer is certainly not to inform God of anything, for God knows all that there is to know, and Jesus taught against ongoing repetition or meaningless discourse in prayer. Spending time in prayer as if there is a need to brief God of the situation would fall under either category. But this isn't what is driving the question for most. Instead, it is a subtle determinism that has entered into our thinking. We think to ourselves, "God is going to do what God is going to do, so why pray?"

The first part of this is true; God *is* going to execute his will. It's the "why pray?" part that is misguided, for what God *has* willed to do is take our prayers into account. He has chosen to invest his power and channel his strength in direct relation to people calling out to him. A deterministic mindset that fosters prayerlessness gives into a half-truth, which results in a falsehood. What God has chosen is to have the prayers of people like you and me factor into what he does. He has *chosen* to have our prayers matter. God has determined to have our communication with him factor into his decision-making process.

This raises the dynamic of divine providence. The Latin term from which we get our word *providence* means to "oversee" a thing, to "be in charge." Divine providence is God's care for his creation, preserving it in existence and guiding it to his intended ends. Providence is often misunderstood. The idea of providence means that we are able to live in the assurance that God is present and active in our lives. All of creation is being *preserved* by God—he maintains and sustains it—and all of creation is being *governed* by God as he guides and directs the course of events to fulfill his purposes. Creation was God's originating work; providence reflects his ongoing relationship with his creation. As Paul wrote to the Colossians, "in him all things hold together" (Colossians 1:17).

So providence wars against the idea of deism, which is often behind the "Why pray?" mentality. Deism maintains that once God made the world and established its various patterns of action, he simply turned it loose to run on its own. Like a well-designed clock, God "wound up" the world and set it on the mantle to operate. Not so—at least according to the Bible, which maintains that the creation would cease to *be* apart from God's continued involvement. Creation has no inherent power of its own to exist. Rather than a wound-up clock, a better idea is that of a power tool that needs God's finger on the button to keep it operating, or a car needing God's foot on the gas pedal. Poor analogies, but they are more true to the idea of providence than the absentee, detached God of deism.

Into this theological mix comes prayer. We are commanded to pray, and encouraged that our prayers will have great effect (James 5:16). Rather than two things diametrically opposed to one another, God works in a partnership or union with our prayers. Prayer is often the means by which God chooses to do what he is going to do in and through his providence. It is the means he has willed for his ends. So God's activity and your activity are not mutually exclusive. God will accomplish his ends, but he has chosen to do so by employing means to those ends—often the means of human agency—including prayer. So while prayer brings us in line with God's purposes, it also contributes to God's purposes, even purposes set before time began (for God himself is outside of time). As C. S. Lewis writes:

> When we are praying the thought will often cross our minds that (if we only knew it) the event is already decided one way or the other. I believe this to be no good reason for ceasing our prayers, though the event certainly has been decided in a sense—it was decided "before all worlds." But one of the things that really caused it to happen may be this very prayer that we are now offering.

So the Bible says, without blushing, "You do not have, because you do not ask God" (James 4:2). I know that there are many times I have something that I need to be praying about or a need that could use God's supernatural assistance, but I really don't end up praying about it very much. Just a little mental prayer here and there, shot up as an afterthought. But then, in an effort to get help, I turn around and spend enormous amounts of energy reading self-help books, going to seminars, listening to tapes or talking to people. When this occurs, I'm giving in to a functional deism. If I shrug my shoulders and feel that while I should pray, it probably won't make much of a difference—God is going to do what God is going to do—then I'm giving in to a functional determinism. Neither reflects the relationship God is inviting us to experience through prayer.

So does it matter how *much* you labor over something in prayer? Does it matter how many times you pray, or for how long you bring it before God? Yes.

Not in the sense of long, rambling prayers which go on and on with mere repetition—"And when you pray, do not keep on babbling like pagans," Jesus warned, "for they think they will be heard because of their many words" (Matthew 6:7)—but in terms of regularly, faithfully, bringing things before God that matter to you. If you do not seem to care, why should God? This is why large numbers of people praying about something matters. If the prayer of a single person impresses God and is taken into consideration, what then of five, fifty or five hundred praying? It isn't that prayer forces God's hand, as if the more people you have praying, the more God has to do what is being asked; it's simply that God has willed to take our prayers into account, so we pray in the faith that it matters.

Even for daily bread.

SIX

Honest

*"Forgive us our debts,
as we also have forgiven our debtors."*

Whatever became of sin?

This was the question posed by psychologist Karl Menninger, who painstakingly detailed our collective loss of any sense of personal wrongdoing, exploring how the theological notion of sin became the legal idea of crime and then slid further from its true meaning when it was relegated to the psychological category of sickness.

In truth, nothing has become of sin. It is alive and well, though we work hard to remove its sting from our thinking. Steven Schwartz writes that we work hard to make *lust* "sensuality," *greed* "resource management optimization" and *anger* "being honest with your emotions." *Pride*, of course, is "asserting your self-worth," and *envy* is that which fuels "the spirit of healthy competition." Dorothy Sayers ruthlessly exposes this semantic sleight of hand by noting that a person "may be greedy and selfish; spiteful, cruel, jealous, and unjust; violent and brutal; grasping, unscrupulous, and a liar; stubborn and arrogant; stupid, morose, and dead to every noble instinct—and still we are ready to say of him that he is not an immoral man."

Or at least we will not say it of ourselves.

Yet this is precisely what Jesus teaches us to do, admonishing us to pray, "Forgive us our debts, as we also have forgiven our debtors." Debt is a Jewish way of speaking about sin. Since we do not have an English word that can serve in this way, early English translator John Knox used the word *trespasses* even though the Vulgate kept the Jewish *debita*.

So prayer must be honest. Being honest when we talk to God means that we don't try to conceal who we are, what we have done or the choices that we have made—much less what it means for our relationship with God. Imagine assaulting a friend in an unconscionable fashion, and the next day meeting him or her for coffee as if nothing happened. It would be ridiculous to assume anything relational could go forward without addressing the wrong that had been done. Because of our sin, not all is right between us and God, and it is through prayer that we address what is wrong.

So we are to pray, regularly, for forgiveness. "As bread is the first need of the body," writes Andrew Murray, "so forgiveness is for the soul."

Some wonder why this is necessary. Were we not forgiven of our sins when we became Christians? Why do we need to continue to seek forgiveness? Is our original salvation and forgiveness dependent on continually seeking forgiveness?

It is important not to confuse the sinful state in which we come to Christ for salvation and the sin we subsequently commit as Christ followers. Christians have experienced God's once-for-all forgiveness through their acceptance of Christ's work on the cross. This is a *positional* forgiveness, moving us from death to life. This does not need to be repeated. However there is a *relational* forgiveness that is called for as an ongoing part of our new life in Christ. Whereas positional forgiveness came from standing before God as *Judge*, relational forgiveness is called for as we stand before God as *Father.*

The washing of the disciples' feet pictures this well. Peter did not want his feet washed, but Jesus insisted. Then Peter wanted a full bath, but that was unnecessary. "Dirt on the feet symbolizes the daily surface contamination from sin that we experience as we walk through life," writes John MacArthur. "It does not, and cannot, make us entirely dirty, because we have been permanently cleansed from that. The positional purging of salvation . . . needs no repetition, but the practical purging is needed every day, because every day we fall short of God's perfect holiness." As Jesus himself stated, "Unless I wash you, you have no part with me" (John 13:8). The spiritual cleansing that comes from seeking daily forgiveness is decisive for maintaining our "part" with Jesus, meaning an ongoing relationship of intimacy.

This is more important than many of us realize.

Confession is what enables our prayers to go to God unencumbered. The prophet Isaiah proclaimed to the people:

> Your iniquities have separated
>   you from your God;
> your sins have hidden his face from you,
>   so that he will not hear. (Isaiah 59:2)

Unconfessed, unrepentant sin cuts off our communication with God. If we are tolerating ongoing patterns of sin in our life, rationalizing them away and refusing to repent, we shouldn't waste our breath praying unless it is a prayer of confession.

This aspect of prayer is not blithely saying "God, forgive me for all of my sins" and then moving on to the next item of business. There is a sense that we are to take some time and be specific about what sins we are confessing and seeking forgiveness *for.* Not only is this suggested by asking forgiveness for debts (plural) but also in how the request to be forgiven is tied to specific acts of horizontal, relational forgiveness toward others.

Forgiveness toward others is unnervingly specific; the corollary is that seeking forgiveness from God is similarly specific: "God, forgive me for looking long and hard at the woman in the store today and catering to sexual thoughts; forgive me for lying to my coworker about the project deadline; forgive me for blowing up in anger at my son; forgive me for tearing down that person's reputation." This is not pursued in some kind of morbid self-flagellation but rather in authentic confession. We don't commit our sins in some bland, generic manner, and we shouldn't confess them that way either.

This means that when we pray, there should be a time of quiet introspection; time where we scroll through the day or the hours that preceded our time of prayer and allow the Holy Spirit to prompt our confession. When I am quiet before him, many things come blazing into my mind that I need to own up to before God.

But is there more to authentic confession than list-making and acknowledgment?

Yes, if it is to be true repentance.

King David experienced one of the most dramatic moral breakdowns in human history, beginning with voyeurism, moving into adultery and ending with murder. His prayer of confession, which was accepted by God as such, reveals what should be manifest in ours, beginning with regret:

> Have mercy on me, O God,
> > according to your unfailing love;
> according to your great compassion
> > blot out my transgressions.
> Wash away all my iniquity
> > and cleanse me from my sin.
> For I know my transgressions,
> > and my sin is always before me. (Psalm 51:1-3)

Regret is one of the more slippery stages of spiritual life to navigate. While it is certainly the first component of prayerfully seeking forgiveness, that is all it is: the first step. And regret is usually only circumstance deep because it is often about the consequences of getting caught or being revealed. If it stops there, that's all it is—regret because of negative *consequences*. With regret there are few if any *relational* issues being addressed, but relationships are at the heart of any prayer for forgiveness.

A few years ago I was traveling abroad and was told of a well-known man in the country I was visiting who lost his position due to a long-term extramarital affair. A friend of mine was asked to help mediate the situation in order to determine how the man might be restored. The first question my friend asked was, "Did the man come forward, of his own accord, to confess and own what he did in order to seek help, or was he simply discovered?" This is an extremely insightful and important question. Regret alone is insufficient for restoration, for it leaves out the larger question of remorse, which is where David's confessional odyssey journeyed next.

> Against you, you only, have I sinned
>   and done what is evil in your sight,
> so that you are proved right when you speak
>   and justified when you judge.
> Surely I was sinful at birth,
>   sinful from the time my mother conceived me.

Surely you desire truth in the inner parts;
>   you teach me wisdom in the inmost place. (Psalm 51:4-6)

Take a moment with this Scripture; count the number of times David talks directly *to* God, *about* God and about his relationship *with* God in those few lines. "Against *you* I have sinned. I've done what is evil in *your* sight. This is about what *you* speak, what *you* judge; it's about *your* truth and *your* wisdom."

For David, confession wasn't simply about the wreck he had made of his life, but the wreck he had made of his relationship with *God*. This is the difference between regret and remorse. Remorse is about sorrow. Not just sorrow over what's happened to your life but what you did wrong in the eyes of God: that your sin was a personal affront to his nature, character and name; that you have driven a wedge between yourself and God, and the separation is more than your heart can bear because you love him, and nothing matters more than your relationship with him.

Remorse is not just grief over what you have done to your life, but for what you have done to your life with God. This is the truth that David knew from his inmost parts, and in prayer he offered it from his inmost parts to God.

But even remorse is not the end of the journey. Repentance is.

Cleanse me with hyssop, and I will be clean;
>   wash me, and I will be whiter than snow.
Let me hear joy and gladness;

let the bones you have crushed rejoice.
Hide your face from my sins
    and blot out my iniquity.
Create in me a pure heart, O God,
    and renew a steadfast spirit within me.
Do not cast me from your presence
    or take your Holy Spirit from me.
Restore to me the joy of your salvation
    and grant me a willing spirit, to sustain me.

Then I will teach transgressors your ways,
    and sinners will turn back to you.
Save me from bloodguilt, O God,
    the God who saves me,
    and my tongue will sing of your righteousness.
O Lord, open my lips,
    and my mouth will declare your praise.
You do not delight in sacrifice, or I would bring it;
    you do not take pleasure in burnt offerings.
The sacrifices of God are a broken spirit;
    a broken and contrite heart,
    O God, you will not despise. (Psalm 51:7-17)

Repentance is the English translation of *metanoia*, a rich word in
the Greek language that carries the idea of heading in one direction, realizing that it is the wrong way and then turning around to-

ward the *right* direction. More than regret, beyond even remorse, repentance involves a resolve to turn *away* from the sin. This is the prayer that truly seeks forgiveness and receives it.

This is a matter of determination. I can regret a lie and have remorse over what it means to my intimacy with God. Yet neither state speaks to whether I will attempt to avoid the same lying pattern tomorrow. In many ways this is what prevents cheap forgiveness, the "sinning so grace may abound" silliness that could set up residence in anyone's spiritual life. Yes, if we sin, we can seek forgiveness, but forgiveness involves regret, remorse and *repentance*. Apart from this journey, there is no *true* prayer for the forgiveness of our debts.

But there is an even more unsettling dynamic to this prayer; our prayers for forgiveness are evaluated by how we forgive *others*. Chrysostom writes that in his day there were many who suppressed this clause of the Lord's Prayer altogether. I don't blame them, yet I know of no other way to read the teaching of Jesus. Those who say that this simply means that we must be in a forgiving mood or we will not *seek* forgiveness dilute the force of the text.

We are all too prone to ask for forgiveness when we ourselves are unwilling to forgive. This was the point of Jesus' story of the unmerciful servant who was forgiven much by the king but who refused to forgive another his own debt (Matthew 18:21-35). As C. S. Lewis once suggested, we all think forgiveness is a wonderful idea until we actually have someone to forgive. No, the weight of

Jesus' teaching must remain. As John Stott writes, "God forgives only the penitent and . . . one of the chief evidences of true penitence is a forgiving spirit." Or as George Herbert said, "He that cannot forgive others, breaks the bridge over which he himself must pass if he would ever reach heaven."

Our tendency is to make the prayer of forgiveness a personal, individualized affair between ourself and God. God insists on bringing others into the picture; not simply those we have offended through our sins but also those that have offended us. As Augustine reminded, "In no other petition do we pray in such a manner as to make a kind of covenant with the Lord, for we say, 'Forgive us as we also forgive.'"

This is hard. Particularly, forgiving those who do not themselves feel the *need* to be forgiven. There are people walking in and through my life that I feel terribly wronged by who have never asked for my forgiveness. Indeed, if I were to bring the matter up, they may very well respond that I need to ask forgiveness of them.

And everything within me wants to meet their spirit in like manner. Yet as Chrysostom maintained, "Nothing makes us so like God as our readiness to forgive the wicked and the wrongdoer."

Yet such forgiveness should not be misconstrued. Lewis Smedes informs us that there are two things forgiveness does not always require: reunion and restoration. You can forgive someone and welcome them back into the community of people you interact with, but that does not mean that you necessarily welcome them back into your most intimate group of friends and family, much less be subject to their wrongdoing in the future. When a person wrongs us, they have erected a barrier between us and them. The most obvious barrier is the sense of being violated—which is what makes us angry, hostile or full of resentment. This is the primary obstacle that forgiveness removes. But only the person we are choosing to forgive can remove the second obstacle, and this depends on whether or not they are willing to address the wrong that was done.

During the South African conflict over apartheid, Bishop Desmond Tutu gave a speech titled "We Forgive You." In that speech he drew a line between forgiveness and reunion. "If I have stolen your pen, I can't really be contrite when I say, 'Please forgive me' if at the same time I still keep your pen. If I am truly repentant, then I will demonstrate this genuine repentance by returning your pen." Tutu was saying, in effect, "I forgive you for stealing from me. And my forgiveness does not depend on you doing or promising anything. You can even continue on as a professional thief. But for my forgiveness to also become a relational reunion, I want back what you stole. And I need to be assured that you will not steal from me again. Else I will forgive, but I will not leave you alone with my property. I will, and must, draw that boundary." As Paul wrote to Timothy, "[There are people who are] without love and unforgiving. . . . Have nothing to do with them" (2 Timothy 3:3, 5).

As I write, I am emerging from a season of deep testing—and a fair degree of failure—in this very area. Some people who were very close to me did more than betray me; they assaulted me in ways that I would have considered unimaginable, and I was caught wholly off-guard by both their spirit and actions. One has yet to seek forgiveness for any aspect of the ordeal or even betray any sense that they should.

Another sought reconciliation. Having once heard me speak of Tutu's "pen" speech, she presented me with her favorite pen. Taped to its sides were the handwritten words *Love, Trust* and *Loyalty.* The very three things she knew I felt had been stripped of our relationship. She was offering them back.

The truth is that I didn't want them back. I didn't want to be reconciled. Yet she forced the swirling waters of resentment and bitterness—fueled by actions that screamed out for justification—to stand before the uncompromising stare of grace.

I took the pen.

Richard Foster wisely writes that while we may not cease to hurt or forget, we must forgive, which means "we no longer use the memory against others." This is not primarily an emotional act—few could pass that test—but an act of the will. It is a determination. This makes forgiving others a *process.* Most who have written on it extensively would agree. And it is an emotionally confusing process, with anger frequently erupting in our souls along the way. It is not like flipping a light switch, though I wish that were the case.

There are some individuals I have worked a lifetime to forgive (and must continue to do so, it seems). I find myself needing to forgive over and over again for events buried in the past that continue to thrust themselves on my psyche. I come to a place where I think I have truly forgiven someone, and then a memory returns, a sentence is remembered, a face is seen, and the old wound is re-opened and resentment floods my emotions. The feelings of anger, bitterness and rage are as fresh as if it had happened the day before, in seeming mockery of the days, weeks, months and even years I had spent praying for a forgiving spirit.

Jesus was once asked about the number of times someone should be forgiven. Should it be seven? This would have been considered most generous and far beyond the bounds of common spirituality. Jesus replied, "No, seventy times seven." C. S. Lewis said that forgiving others seventy times seven may not be for 490 separate offenses, but perhaps 490 times for the same one. In *Letters to Malcolm* he writes of finally reaching a sense of forgiveness for someone he had been trying to forgive for thirty years. Later, in a letter to a friend, he revealed that the person he had at last forgiven was the cruel schoolmaster who so darkened his childhood. So as we journey, we should not fall prey to the paranoia that unless we have made sufficient progress, we will not receive God's forgiveness. Jesus is not teaching that we earn forgiveness by forgiving others. That would go against the heart of his teaching on grace and undermine the good news Jesus came to announce. Forgiveness from God hinges not on my "arrival" at forgiving others but on my active commitment to the *process* of forgiving others. The key is *striving* to forgive.

So we constantly stay in forgiveness mode. Then we can come before God and ask him to do the same for us.

SEVEN

Humble

"And lead us not into temptation,
but deliver us from the evil one."

 here are two equal and opposite errors into which our race can fall about the devils," wrote C. S. Lewis in one of his better-known reflections. "One is to disbelieve in their existence. The other is to believe, and to feel an excessive and unhealthy interest in them. They themselves," adds Lewis, "are equally pleased by both errors."

Jesus' teaching on prayer seems to caution us most against the *first* of these errors.

The spiritual realm is, of course, real. Which means the world of the occult is real. I know that is not the most comforting sentence to read, but it is true. When I have encountered the demonic, I have been overwhelmed by the hatred, the evil, the bone-chilling . . . well, *chill*. I have never been able to determine whether the temperature actually drops or the presence of such spirits simply creates a deeply disturbing effect that is similar to teeth-chattering cold.

At this point it is customary to declare, for those easily disturbed by such matters, that greater is *he* that is in you than he that is in the world. Yes, but he that is in the world is greater than *you*. That is why Jesus instructed us to pray *not,* you will notice, for dominance (which tempers the presumptive bravado among some Christians in their abilities against demons) but for deliverance. Were it not for the protective power of the Holy Spirit and the work of the angels, I do not believe a single Christian would live to see the dawn, for the evil one is truly malevolent.

For this reason, the final note in a prayer's song is in the key of humility, and it rings out through a single instrument—reality. Jesus taught us to pray for deliverance because we are not able to stand up to the onslaught of the evil one on our own. Nor should we ever think we can. Only through prayer can we survive the spiritual warfare swirling around our lives, much less wage a frontal assault.

There: now that we are sobered up a bit, let's examine prayer in regard to temptation. We have been directed to pray for our past (forgiveness), our present (bread) and now our future (temptation and evil). The wording of this part of prayer has raised many questions, not the least of which, "So God leads us to temptation, and we must ask him not to? What kind of God is that?"

Most would quickly say, "No, God does not tempt anyone," and they would be right. James writes:

When tempted, no one should say, "God is tempting me."
For God cannot be tempted by evil, nor does he tempt anyone; but each one is tempted when, by his own evil desire,
he is dragged away and enticed. Then, after desire has con-
ceived, it gives birth to sin; and sin, when it is full-grown,
gives birth to death. (James 1:13-15)

But that is not what Jesus said to pray about. He also is not suggesting that we are to pray that we would not be led to a *place* of
temptation or to be allowed to be tempted, both of which God
seems very open to allowing. Jesus himself was led by the Holy
Spirit into the wilderness for this very purpose. The wording of
Matthew is explicit: "Jesus was led by the Spirit into the desert to
be tempted by the devil" (Matthew 4:1). And God certainly gave
Satan a shot at the Old Testament saint Job.

So through a process of elimination, letting the Bible interpret
the Bible on such matters (always the best approach), it would
seem that to pray that God would not lead us into temptation ad-
dresses two needs: (1) that we would not find ourselves subject to
anything that would unduly test our mettle, and (2) that we would
not find ourselves in a state where we do not have the mettle for
the test. Since God has promised that we will not be tempted beyond what we can bear (1 Corinthians 10:13), we can certainly
pray to that end.

More pressing, we are to pray that we would be able to bear that

which *is* within our capabilities. Much temptation comes our way
that to resist demands *all* that we have, and we have that *all*, but
only through prayer. Too many Christians claim God's promise regarding the limits of temptation as a sort of safety net: "Not to
worry. God won't put me in over my head." They mistakenly read
this promise in light of their natural abilities instead of their supernatural abilities. Our ability to resist temptation is not based on
our life apart from Christ but our Spirit-filled life *in* Christ. If, in
step with our life in Christ, we do not pray for God's deliverance
from temptation, we shouldn't expect the deliverance that we
could have had. The promise for a "way out" of temptation is kept
through the prayer to avoid the situation to begin with. "Watch
and pray," Jesus admonished the disciples in Gethsemane, "so that
you will not fall into temptation. The spirit is willing, but the body
is weak" (Matthew 26:41).

Every day I will be tempted to do things that will "embarrass"
God, that will move me away from him rather than closer to him.
Left to myself, I will succumb. So I am in desperate need of God's
help to live the way I am supposed to live, and I am to ask him for
help to do it.

While this request is highly significant, humility goes beyond
just praying the prayer. When I pray that I would not be led into
temptation, I am acknowledging that I am susceptible to yielding
to any temptation.

Gordon MacDonald was the senior minister at a large church in

New England before becoming the president of the famed campus ministry InterVarsity Christian Fellowship. Along the way he authored numerous best-selling Christian books. He was asked to give a speech at a college commencement, and before the festivities began, MacDonald spent time with a member of the school's board in the president's office. They began asking each other questions in order to become acquainted, when suddenly the board member raised a provocative question that stood out to MacDonald, and would for years to come: "If Satan were to blow you out of the water, how do you think he would do it?"

"I'm not sure I know," MacDonald answered. "All sorts of ways, I suppose; but I know there's one way he wouldn't get me. He'd never get me in the area of my personal relationships. That's one place where I have no doubt that I'm as strong as you can get."

It wasn't long after that conversation that MacDonald's world broke open, and in the area of the most important personal relationship MacDonald had. He betrayed the covenant of his marriage and became, in his own words, a "broken-world person." When we don't think we are susceptible in a given area, we let down our guard and become more exposed than ever. MacDonald's reflections on his descent into temptation's lair are penetrating: "A chain of seemingly innocent choices became destructive, and it was my fault. Choice by choice by choice, each easier to make, each becoming gradually darker. And then my world broke—in the very area I had predicted I was safe."

The humility inherent in this aspect of prayer involves a keen awareness that no matter what sin and failure I see in the life of another, I must confess that "but by the grace of God, there go I."

We now must return to the demonic. The humility God seeks in our prayer involves asking for deliverance not just from temptation but from the evil one and, I assume, his minions. Older translations often rendered Jesus' words as merely "evil," but it is more accurate to render it *evil one*. We are to seek deliverance from the evil *one*. Satan is known by many names—the devil, Lucifer, the tempter, the deceiver, the adversary and the prince of darkness. The Bible suggests that Satan was a fallen angel who chose to rebel against God, leading at least one-third of the angels with him. He is not omniscient, omnipresent or omnipotent. He is not God or even close to being God. He is not the evil twin brother of Jesus. He is, at most, an angel who fell. No more, no less.

The story seems to be that Satan gave in to pride, wanting to sit where God sits, rebelling against God and declaring all-out war. The Bible doesn't go into detail about why God allowed Satan to be in opposition to him. All we know is that God has allowed Satan to exercise his free will to rebel, just as he has allowed us to freely make choices.

Regardless of what *we* may think, Jesus believed in Satan's existence. He didn't think he was a myth. He didn't think he was a figment of someone's imagination or some cartoon character from a can of "deviled" ham. Jesus didn't think Satan was a mere projection of the human mind to explain the mysteries of evil. Jesus believed him to be a real, live spiritual being. He took Satan very seriously and wanted his followers to take him seriously as well. Jesus called Satan a murderer (John 8:44), one who kills and destroys. Satan has been a murderer "from the beginning," Jesus said, no doubt referring to the spiritual death of Adam and Eve, and soon thereafter the physical murder of Abel.

Jesus also called Satan a liar: "There is no truth in him. When he lies, he speaks his native language, for he is a liar and the father of lies" (John 8:44). The word *devil* is the Greek word *diabolos,* which means slanderer—someone who spreads lies and half-truths about someone or something. It was a term that referred to bringing false charges against someone in order to convict them unjustly. And the word *Satan* means "accuser"—again, one who brings hostile, false accusations against someone else. There is little hidden about the heart of Satan's deceptive agenda. His supreme lie is that bad is good, wrong is right and what is harmful is healthy. His ultimate lie is that choosing to sin—regardless of the sin itself—is best.

In one of Jesus' many stories, that of the sower and the seed, he also referred to Satan functioning as a destroyer (Luke 8:4-15). When a seed falls to the ground, there is much that can keep it from taking root. As a spiritual subversive Satan wants to keep everyone away from the truth of God's message through Christ. When people *do* hear the message of Christ, jogging their souls awake, Satan does everything possible to have them go back to sleep by dismissing the truth from their lives. He knows it is a sleep they may never awaken from. In fact, that is the goal. If he can't steal it from their hearts, he will try to have it remain dormant—for another time and place.

About now, you may be thinking, *Yes, but isn't he defeated?* We do not want the lion, Satan, prowling around, waiting to devour us (though this is precisely what the Bible describes), but a humiliated, even comical character that we can dismiss with the lightest of prayers on our lips and a wave of our hand. This, though, is not the true state of affairs. Do you recall the disciples returning to Jesus in defeat, unable to exorcise one person (Mark 9:14-29)? This was Peter, for goodness sake, along with James and John. Apostles. Jesus gave them the sobering reminder that the spiritual realm is real, that evil and the evil one are strong, and that only through serious prayer could there be victory.

But Satan is defeated. A week before his death Jesus told his disciples, "'The time of judgment for the world has come, when [Satan] will be cast out'" (John 12:31 NLT). The death and resurrection of Jesus accomplished the defeat of Satan. Sin and death do not have the final victory for those in Christ. We have received forgiveness for our sins; we walk in a new relationship with God; and when we die, we enter into life eternal. And at the end of time, when Jesus returns, Satan will be judged along with everyone else. A small girl once asked one of my professors in seminary, "Why doesn't God just pinch the devil's head off?" My old mentor thought a moment, and then responded, "He will."

But that act is for another day, so we are to pray.

Because for now, *we need to be delivered.*

EIGHT

Our Struggle with
Unanswered Prayer

But go to him when your need is desperate, when all other help is vain,
and what do you find? A door slammed in your face, and a sound of
bolting and double bolting on the inside. After that, silence. . . .

Why is he so present a commander in our time of prosperity and
so very absent a help in time of trouble?

C. S. LEWIS

What happens when we pray?

Jesus has taught us to pray, but we don't always get what we pray for. The daily bread seems absent from our table in so many ways, and we are racked by hunger pangs.

We pray, and there's no answer.

We pray, and nothing happens.

We pray, and things stay the same.

We pray, and it feels as if we might as well have been talking to the wall.

Or so it seems.

We know what *can* happen, at least in terms of possibility; there is a God on the loose who breathed the entire universe into being. But what actually *does* occur?

Three things: God *hears,* God *cares,* and God *answers.* Every time, for every person, for every prayer.

GOD HEARS

First, God *hears.* When you talk to God, he is listening. In 1 John, the Bible says in no uncertain terms that "This is the con-fidence we have in approaching God: . . . he hears us" (1 John 5:14). The declaration is unambiguous. When we pray, our words never fall on deaf ears. Whether by spoken word, ritual or quiet anguish, prayer ascends without encumbrance to the very throne room of God. The Lord's Prayer suggests that only an unforgiving spirit can impede the efficacy of prayer. Yet even that dire moment can be quickly addressed; indeed, should be at the onset of *every* prayer.

Some have wondered whether God hears the prayers of those who are *not* in relationship with him. Does he hear only Christian prayers? What of the person of Jewish or Muslim faith? This ques-tion is posed in light of our pluralistic world where one faith is often seen as equivalent to another. The quick answer frequently is, "of course God hears every prayer."

Actually, it depends.

God hears all prayers that are prayed to him as God, regardless of who prays them. But notice the wording: as long as they are prayed to him *as God*. Does God hear the prayer of a man who knowingly disavows God's self-revelation in the Bible—and supremely in Christ—for the worship of a fertility goddess? Is the prayer to that goddess heard by the God of the Bible as prayer to him? Of course not, for it is not prayer to him *as* God. He is aware of the man's life and words, but that doesn't mean they are taken as prayer to him, much less heard in the context of the relationship enjoyed between God and a fully adopted son or daughter who has come to him as a believer.

We must avoid the nonsense that the God of the Bible is one and the same as the god of a fertility cult, with all ideas of deity melding together into some being devoid of definition. We can assert with confidence that God has—as Jesus began his teaching on prayer—a *name*. He knows who he is, and who he is not. Not all prayer is addressed to him. Of course, any prayer someone outside of a relationship with God may one day direct toward him *as* the one, true, living God would be instantly received as such, but any imagined offerings to a pagan goddess would not be.

This begs the question of the person who cries out to God but fails to have the theological or biblical literacy to do so properly. This is an altogether different matter, and becomes a question of the heart's intent. God is, and will be, the perfect Judge of such situations. Any and all prayer authentically intended for God as God, no matter how theologically illiterate or uninformed the person may be, is heard by God.

So we have a God with a strong bias toward *listening*.

GOD CARES

But not only does God hear our prayers, he *cares* about them. The apostle Peter writes, "Let him [God] have all your worries and cares, for he is always thinking about you and watching everything that concerns you" (1 Peter 5:7 LB). Notice the emphasis: God is concerned not simply with his grand plan but with our cares and concerns.

When it comes to our life, God's empathy knows no bounds. Empathy is an important word, not to be confused (as it commonly is) with sympathy. *Sympathy* is feeling sorry for someone. *Empathy* is feeling what the other person feels. We pray to an empathetic God, if for no other reason than Christ, our mediator, is ensuring it. Speaking of Jesus, the writer of Hebrews maintains that "we do not have a high priest who is unable to empathize with our weaknesses, but we have one who has been tempted in every way, just as we are." Then the writer goes on: "Let us then approach God's throne of grace with confidence, so that we may receive mercy and find grace to help us in our time of need" (Hebrews 4:15-16 TNIV).

You are not bothering him, much less trying his patience, with your prayers. You matter to him, and what matters to you matters to him. God gave you your feelings, so he is not offended by them. Contrary to what you may have thought, they are precious to him.

GOD ANSWERS

Finally, God *answers* every prayer. There is no such thing as unanswered prayer. Now some of you reading these words may have just found yourself shaking your head in disbelief. You know this is not true, and you have the list to prove it. But let's speak the truth. What we often have is a list of prayers that were not answered the way we *desired*. God *answers* every prayer; *how* he chooses to answer is another matter. We read in the book of Job:

> Why do you complain to him
>   that he answers none of man's words?
> For God does speak—now one way, now another—
>   though man may not perceive it. (Job 33:13-14)

That is the issue: our *perception*.

WHEN GOD SAYS NO

So how might God answer our prayers in a way we may not perceive? The *yes* we can identify; what else is there? The first is the most obvious. Sometimes God's answer is simply *no*. What we ask for, no matter how well-intentioned, could be inappropriate, adverse to optimal kingdom advance or less than fully loving to our lives. Thus God refuses to grant what we have asked. We often refuse to listen to this answer. When no has been given, we often tell ourselves that God simply hasn't answered yet. It is often beyond our thinking to imagine God denying our requests, even though the Bible is full of such responses.

Once Jesus and his followers were traveling to Jerusalem. One of the cities they journeyed through was Samaria; so some went ahead to arrange a place with local inhabitants for Jesus and the others to stay. What happened next is interesting:

> The people there did not welcome him. . . . When the disciples James and John saw this, they asked, "Lord, do you want us to call fire down from heaven to destroy them?" (Luke 9:53-54)

Here were two men who were very sincere in what they were suggesting. They felt that the request made perfect sense in terms of what had transpired. The request was heard; Jesus cared deeply about their concerns. But did Jesus call down the fires of heaven?

Not exactly.

"Jesus turned on them, 'Of course not!' " (Luke 9:55 *The Message*).

God cares deeply about us and hears every request, but that doesn't mean the answer can't be no. This becomes particularly clear to me when I think of my role as a father. Nobody loves my children more than I do. But sometimes when they ask for something, the answer must be—for *their* sake, or the sake of the family—a firm and deliberate no. More times than not, they don't have a clue as to why. It makes perfect sense to their minds to stay up all night, to eat pizza for every meal, to invest significant amounts of our financial resources in the local mall, and to establish a secondary residence in Orlando. I've seen this lessen as they mature. Their requests are more informed as they learn to apply the values they have been raised by. Yet even so, they continue to make requests that reflect pockets of immaturity and require a *no* response.

And still it's hard for them to see why.

This idea is carried throughout the Bible: God said no to Moses when he asked to die in order to be released from the exasperations of pastoral leadership (Numbers 11:15), and again refused him when he asked to enter the Promised Land (Deuteronomy 3:23-26). God said no to Saul when he asked about the Philistines (1 Samuel 28:6); he said no to David's request that he spare his son by Bathsheba (2 Samuel 12:15-18). God said no to Elijah's request to die (something about leading God's people makes you suicidal; 1 Kings 19:1-5); he said no to the prayer of Salome, James and John regarding who would sit at the right and left of Jesus (Matthew 20:20-23).

So it is with our souls in relation to prayer. We often make requests that cannot be granted. Yet we can be assured that God's operative stance toward us is shameless devotion. Even when pain erupts, tragic events continue or requests are denied, we can rest assured that we have been granted a greater blessing—or kept from a deeper, more lasting pain. This can sound trite; it's not. I'm journeying through my fifth decade, and its truth is more essential to my life now than ever before. It is the anchor in the storm. I have finally lived long enough to look back and see its inescapable truth.

But God's no is seldom left to itself. When Paul repeatedly begged God for his "thorn in the flesh" to be removed, the answer was no, but there was more: "[God] said to me, 'My grace is sufficient for you, for my power is made perfect in weakness'" (2 Corinthians 12:9). The purpose behind God's refusal and the ramifications it holds for our life are always coupled with the direct presence and power of God. The fullest sense of God's reply is, "The answer is no, but that just means a different story is going to unfold that you can't foresee; but rest assured, I will be in that story, and it will be OK. Trust me."

WHEN GOD SAYS NOT NOW

But too much is often made of prayer being a yes or no proposition. No is not the only response from God to our prayers when the answer is not an immediate and unmistakable yes. God can also say "not now." When we ask God for something, we are looking for it at once. We have a predetermined timetable. Yet it is sensible to consider that God's answer might be, "this is not a yes or no—it's a 'not now'—the timing is neither right nor best." What makes this so difficult is how saturated our lives have become with instant gratification. We can't imagine a life without express lanes, ATMs, faxes, microwaves, e-mail and instant messaging. We're used to getting what we want when we want it, which makes *later* or *not now* only slightly easier to hear than no.

But God's delay should not be confused with God's denial, much less his silence. He always has reasons for saying not now, and we should greet such delays with trust and patience. Even expectation. Consider *The Message* paraphrase of Romans 8:24: "Waiting does not diminish us, any more than waiting diminishes a pregnant mother. We are enlarged in the waiting." Besides, we may not be ready for what God will say. The delay may have less to do with the timing of events than the timing of our soul's growth. Dallas Willard writes that we may have so little clarity on what a word from God should be like, and so little competence in dealing with it, that such a word would only add to our confusion, even "when it would otherwise be entirely appropriate and helpful."

This raises a dilemma for sincere pray-ers; when are we to *desist*, and when are we to *persist*? When should we take no for no, and when should we commit to laboring in prayer for an answer that is in the not yet category? Or maybe it's a yes, but only through lengthy petition? We have all heard of those receiving what they prayed for after *years* of divine dialogue. Paul seemed to know it was time to give up on his "thorn in the flesh" prayer after three sessions. In truth, praying "three times" was a Hebrew idiom that intimates Paul prayed in every way possible. Yet there was still a sense that he knew it was time to hear God's no. Daniel, however, continued in prayer for three weeks without an answer, and at the point of despair he was informed by an angel that it was his labor that broke the impasse in the spiritual war between the angels. It's safe to say he was glad he stuck with it after the first two weeks.

While there is no easy answer to this dynamic, and it is most often worked out in the depth of intimacy that prayer itself provides, there's more in the Bible about persistence in prayer than quick cessation. There is an interesting turn of the Greek in James 5:17, which, speaking of Elijah, literally reads, "in prayer he prayed." It is commonly translated along the lines of "he prayed earnestly." But the original language suggests that someone might be "in prayer" without praying, meaning he or she didn't *labor* in prayer. It could very well be that the not now of delay may only be breached through the labor of the pray-er that seeks the answer.

I am often shamed by the stories of those saints who prayed for hours each day—the Luthers, Muellers and Wesleys. I identify more with Teresa of Ávila who confessed:

> Very often I was more occupied with the wish to see the end of my hour for prayer. I used to actually watch the sandglass. And the sadness that I sometimes felt on entering my prayer-chapel was so great that it required all my courage to force myself inside.

Yet she is universally recognized as a saint. What marked her life was not the natural proclivity to lengthy prayer but the commitment to praying itself. It may not be *four* hours each morning, but it must be *for* every morning. I think this is the point and practice of labor.

DEEP CALLING TO DEEP

A third response from God that can be mistaken for silence is the most difficult to grasp. At least for me. Perhaps the best way to introduce it is through the words of Psalm 42:

> As the deer pants for streams of water,
>> so my soul pants for you, O God.
> My soul thirsts for God, for the living God. . . .
>
> My tears have been my food day and night,
>> while men say to me all day long,
> "Where is your God?" (Psalm 42:1-3)

Here is someone hungering for a word from God. He alludes to a difficult time, a season where he has been calling out to God in the midst of pain, grief or confusion. From all angles it appears as if God is silent to his cries. But notice what he goes on to say:

> Why are you downcast, O my soul?
>> Why so disturbed within me?
> Put your hope in God. . . .

My soul is downcast within me;

therefore I will remember you. . . .

Deep calls to deep
    in the roar of your waterfalls. (Psalm 42:5-7)

The psalmist comes to see that there is no silence; the answer coming from God is simply deeper than words. God is present and speaking, but what he is saying is not resting on the surface waters of life. This is a season where deep is calling to deep or, as Thomas Kelly phrases it, it is a time of going "down into the recreating silences." So perhaps it's not silence we are encountering while we seek God, but rather a pregnant pause—a prompting to engage in personal reflection so that the deepest of answers, the most profound of responses, can be given and received. In a *Fast Company* article the chess master and much sought-after mentor Bruce Pandolfini discusses how this works with his students:

My lessons consist of a lot of silence. I listen to other teachers, and they're always talking. . . . I let my students think. If I do ask a question and I don't get the right answer, I'll rephrase the question—and wait. I never give the answer. Most of us really don't appreciate the power of silence. Some of the most effective communication—between student and teacher, between master players—takes place during silent periods.

Could this be how God mentors us? Is God's apparent silence the method of a Master Teacher? When I go through seasons where God's answers do not come quickly—but the way God interacts with my prayers draws me into deeper trust, dependence and obedience—the answers I eventually find radically transcend what I initially sought to find.

I get introduced to sin that I need to confront.

I recognize patterns of behavior I need to break.

I gain insights into who I am that I didn't have before.

I discover a depth of relationship with God that I have never before experienced.

I find directional guidance that goes beyond my prayers, often resulting in alterations of the entire trajectory of my life.

There is little doubt, in retrospect, when I have gone through such "deep" times. Without question, they are worth the silence it took to bring them to bear on my life.

Perhaps this is why Kathleen Norris allows her students to make all the noise they want, but then she calls on them to "make silence." The result is certainly similar in spirit. Reflecting on the experience, her elementary-age pupils note that when they were silent, they felt as though they were "waiting for something." One wrote, "Silence is me sleeping waiting to wake up." Perhaps the most profound observation comes from a little girl who said, "Silence reminds me to take my soul with me wherever I go."

Few statements could be more profound. We think of a word

from God as the soul's main sustenance, but silence is a true companion not simply for where it leads but for what it affords: space for God to speak beyond the answers we sought.

"It is no surprise," writes Frederick Buechner, "that the Bible uses hearing, not seeing, as the predominant image for the way human beings know God." Perhaps this deeper communion is behind the concept of *vigils* (waiting), the ancient name for extended prayers given while one might normally be sleeping. It also suggests why the first word of St. Benedict's Rule for monasteries is *listen*. Even before these insights came the ancient desert tradition of Christianity. Alan Jones writes of men and women entering the literal desert even as they embraced a "desert" of the spirit—at once "a place of silence, waiting, and temptation" and "a place of revelation, conversion, and transformation." According to the desert tradition, "empty" places such as the desert were actually full, for in the deadening silence of such experiences, people were known to be reborn.

We can only wonder what his silence holds for us.

As well as the *no,* and *not yet,* and even the *yes.*

For make no mistake, God is answering.

A Final Word

"Very early in the morning, while it was still dark, Jesus got up, left the house and went off to a solitary place, where he prayed."

MARK 1:35

*J*esus did not simply teach us how to pray, he modeled a life of prayer. Those closest to him noted that "Jesus often slipped away to be alone so he could pray." (Luke 5:16 NCV).

But such prayer is not simply a way of life; it is work. It takes intentional commitment and concentrated effort. This is why prayer is known by the monastics as the *opus Dei*, the "work of God." Prayer is to be our principal vocation. There is nothing of greater importance or more vital investment. Which is why Esther de Waal notes in her exploration of Benedictine spirituality, at any hour of prayer (and there are up to seven for the Benedictines each day), "anything else in the monastery must be immediately abandoned: the work of God takes precedence."

But this is not labor in the most common sense of the word, bringing up images of drudgery and fatigue. It is that which liberates our souls for the experience of life itself. Increasingly I see it, or perhaps should say I *experience* it, as Quaker author Douglas Steere has described:

> Prayer . . . is simply a form of waking up out of the dull sleep in which our life has been spent in half-intentions, half-resolutions, half-creations, half-loyalties, and become actively aware of the real character of that which we are and of that which we are over against. It is an opening of drowsy lids. It is a shaking off of grave-clothes. It is a dip into acid. It is a daring to "read the text of the universe in the original."

Prayer is an encounter with God, raw and unfiltered. It is not for the shallow of spirit but for those who wish to plunge head-first into the deep waters of encounter. As Thomas Kelly challenged, "Let us dare to venture together into the inner sanctuary of the soul, where God meets man in awful immediacy." There, and there alone, comes intimacy, transformation and a position in eternity that lifts us into the transcendent in such a way that we can return to the temporal with something the world does not supply.

Yet it remains an event of disarming simplicity.

I rise every morning at 5 a.m. in order to meet with God. During that time, with a large cup of coffee before me, "I lay out the pieces of my life on [his] altar" (Psalm 5:3 *The Message*).

I pray to God as my Father. I imagine him in my mind as Father: loving, encouraging, open, walking with me down an autumn path or a beach with his arm around my shoulder.

I pray to him as the God in heaven, able to act in ways that supersede the petty boundaries of circumstance.

I pray that I would not disappoint him, but would instead please him more this day than the day before.

I force my dreams and passions, sins and failures into the dimensions of his will, while sharing them freely and guileless before his throne.

I pray that I could be used, in whatever way needed, to change the world. That even *this* day might hold a strategic kingdom advance, a new foothold, as heaven grapples with hell for the possession of the world and its inhabitants.

I pray to him as the One who alone gives me my very next breath, as the One who alone is able to forgive.

I pray to him as the One who alone is able to deliver me from the sinful man I most naturally am as well as from the one who seems most naturally intent on my demise.

Along with Douglas Steere, I plead my case with the most measured eloquence, until finally God listens me into silence, into humiliation, into humility, until at last I come into some faint splash of the deep sanity that recalls me to what I am on earth for.

The Lord's Prayer guides this conversation. It informs it, shapes it, challenges it. It holds my prayer accountable, giving it the contours it needs. While seldom spoken verbatim, it always shadows what is.

Yes, all prayer will forever remain shrouded in mystery, for it is deep calling to deep. Paul admitted as much to the Romans: "We do not know what we ought to pray for," and we must rely on "the Spirit himself" to intercede for us in ways "that words cannot express" (Romans 8:26). Yet the words Jesus gave us for prayer are the words that bring our spirits into the conversation and communion needed for the Holy Spirit to take over. "How great, dearest brothers, are the mysteries of the Lord's Prayer," writes Cyprian, "how many, how magnificent, gathered together in a few words, yet abundant in spiritual power. There is nothing whatever with regard to our pleading and our prayer omitted, nothing not contained in this summary of heavenly doctrine."

All I know is that without it I would not know what to pray.

And without prayer I would not be able to live, for prayer truly is the breath of spiritual life, and through it we inhale the very air of eternity.

Suggested Reading

$\mathcal{T}$he following books stand apart from most and will reward any reader's heart, mind, soul and strength. Not all are specifically on prayer, much less the Lord's Prayer (for those titles, see the notes section), but all speak to the life of prayer. Since many come in varying translations and publication dates, only the author and title are cited.

Contemplative Prayer by Thomas Merton

Dimensions of Prayer by Douglas Steere

Interior Castle by Teresa of Ávila

Introduction to the Devout Life by Francis de Sales

Letters to Malcolm: Chiefly on Prayer by C. S. Lewis

The Practice of the Presence by Brother Lawrence

Prayer by Richard J. Foster

Reaching Out by Henri Nouwen

Seeking God: The Way of St. Benedict by Esther de Waal

The Spiritual Life by Evelyn Underhill

A Testament of Devotion by Thomas Kelly

With Christ in the School of Prayer by Andrew Murray

Notes

Introduction: The Prayer We Long For

Page 10: They'd finally asked the right question: The idea of the disciples finally asking the right question was suggested to my thinking by William H. Willimon and Stanley Hauerwas, *Lord, Teach Us: The Lord's Prayer and the Christian Life* (Nashville: Abingdon, 1996), p. 13.

Page 10: "breathing the air of eternity": Evelyn Underhill, "Breathing the Air of Eternity," *Weavings* 17, no. 3 (2002): 8.

Page 11: The Latin tag *lex orandi, lex credendi:* See Geoffrey Wainwright, *Doxology: The Praise of God in Worship, Doctrine, and Life* (New York: Oxford University Press, 1980), p. 218.

Page 11: taught only to converts at baptism: T. W. Manson, "The Lord's Prayer," *Bulletin of the John Rylands Library* 38 (1955-1956): 99-113, 136-48. By the time of Augustine the Lord's Prayer was taught to the catechumens at the conclusion of the catechumenate, in a ceremony that took place one week before the Easter vigil. On this, see W. Harmless, *Augustine and the Catechumenate* (Collegeville, Minn.: Liturgical Press, 1995), p. 286.

Page 13: Here is what Jesus taught: There are two versions of the Lord's Prayer in the New Testament: Matthew 6:9-13 and Luke 11:1-4, with minor differences in the introduction (Matthew's: "This is how you should pray"; Luke's: "When you pray, say") and terminology (e.g., "debts" vs. "transgressions"). Many scholars hold Luke's version to be the older of the two, with Matthew offering a version somewhat enhanced by the already developing liturgical tradition. Or Jesus taught on the matter on more than one occasion, offering minor variations along the way. Regardless, both versions are recorded in the Bible and are marked less by their differences than their virtual congruence. Matthew's version, offered here, is the one universally used by Christians.

Page 14:   The corporate dynamic: The "our" in the first sentence assumes that it is prayed corporately. But too much should not be made of this, because the preceding verses from Jesus focused on the primacy of private prayer.

Page 14:   "Again and again in public and private devotion": Evelyn Underhill, *Practical Mysticism and Abba*, ed. John F. Thornton and Susan B. Varenne (New York: Vintage, 2003), p. 145.

Page 14:   Tertullian's and Augustine's view of the Lord's Prayer: See "Lord's Prayer," *The Oxford Dictionary of the Christian Church,* ed. F. L. Cross and E. A. Livingstone, 3rd ed. (Oxford: Oxford University Press, 1997), p. 996. For the best single-volume overview of how the Lord's Prayer has been treated, see Kenneth W. Stevenson, *The Lord's Prayer* (Minneapolis: Fortress Press, 2004).

Page 14:   Thomas Merton wrote: Thomas Merton, *The Sign of Jonas* (New York: Harcourt, Brace, 1953), p. 198.

Chapter 1: Intimate

Page 17:   John Stott's morning prayer: Cited by John W. Yates III, "Pottering and Prayer," *ChristianityToday.com,* April 27, 2001, <www.christianitytoday.com/ct/2001/005/4.60.html>.

Pages 19-20:   the research of Joachim Jeremias concludes: Joachim Jeremias, *The Prayers of Jesus* (Philadelphia: Fortress Press, 1967), p. 57.

Page 20:   *abba* and *imma:* Ibid., p. 96.

Page 21:   "We make *bold* to say": E. Glenn Hinson, *The Reaffirmation of Prayer* (Nashville: Broadman, 1979), p. 115.

Page 21:   *"audemus quotidie dicere"*: Augustine, cited in Kenneth W. Stevenson, *The Lord's Prayer* (Minneapolis: Fortress Press, 2004), p. 84.

Page 21:   Susan and Lucy rolling in the grass with Aslan: C. S. Lewis, *The Lion, the Witch, and the Wardrobe* (New York: Macmillan, 1950), p. 158.

Page 22:   "it would have been disrespectful": Jeremias, *Prayers of Jesus,* p. 62.

Page 23:   Philip Yancey's observations about God: Philip Yancey, *The Jesus I Never Knew* (Grand Rapids: Zondervan, 1995), pp. 36-38.

Page 24:   "only the words 'Our Father' ": Frederick Buechner, *Whistling in the Dark* (San Francisco: Harper & Row, 1988), p. 77.

Chapter 2: Expectant

Page 29:   "Our Father always near us": Dallas Willard, *The Divine Conspiracy* (New York: HarperSanFrancisco, 1998), p. 257.

Page 29:   C. S. Lewis once observed: C. S. Lewis, *Letters to Malcolm: Chiefly on Prayer* (New York: Harvest, 1964), p. 57.

Chapter 3: Reverent

Page 36:   Andrew Murray on *holy* and *father:* Andrew Murray, *With Christ in the School of Prayer* (Springdale, Penn.: Whitaker House, 1981), p. 32.

Pages 36-37:   Augustine on God's holy name: Augustine *Our Lord's Sermon on the Mount* 5.19, Nicene and Post-Nicene Fathers, ed. Philip Schaff, vol. 6 (Peabody, Mass.: Hendrickson, 1999).

Page 37:   Will Willimon and Stanley Hauerwas write of a college student: William Willimon and Stanley Hauerwas, *Lord, Teach Us* (Nashville: Abingdon, 1996), pp. 48-49.

Page 38:   bishop Cyprian of Carthage wrote: Cyprian, cited in *Matthew 1-13,* Ancient Christian Commentary on Scripture, New Testament 1a, ed. Manlio Simonetti (Downers Grove, Ill.: InterVarsity Press, 2001), p. 132.

Pages 41-42:   "Show me that you are redeemed": Friedrich Nietzsche, cited by

William Barclay, *The Lord's Prayer* (Louisville, Ky.: Westminster John Knox, 1998), p. 50.

Pages 42-43: "Thus the site of Solomon's Temple": Evelyn Underhill, *Practical Mysticism and Abba*, ed. John F. Thornton and Susan B. Varenne (New York: Vintage, 2003), p. 166.

Chapter 4: Submitted

Page 45:   "At that time I was an undergraduate": Paul Little, adapted from Robert B. Munger's 1981 Urbana Student Mission Conference address, "Knowing God's Will," in *Confessing Christ as Lord: The Urbana 81 Compendium*, ed. John W. Alexander (Downers Grove, Ill.: InterVarsity Press, 1982), p. 153. See also Paul Little, *Affirming the Will of God* (Downers Grove, Ill.: InterVarsity Press, 1971).

Page 46:   Søren Kierkegaard on prayer: Søren Kierkegaard, cited by Mortimer Adler and Charles Van Doren, eds., *Great Treasury of Western Thought* (New York: R. R. Bowker, 1977), p. 1360.

Page 47:   Teresa of Ávila on prayer: Teresa of Ávila, *Interior Castle,* ed. and trans. E. Allison Peers (New York: Doubleday, 1989), p. 51.

Page 47:   Origen once counseled: Origen, cited in *Matthew 1-13,* Ancient Christian Commentary on Scripture, New Testament 1a, ed. Manlio Simonetti (Downers Grove, Ill.: InterVarsity Press, 2001), p. 130.

Page 48:   "a silent surrendering of everything to God": Søren Kierkegaard, *Journals* (New York: Oxford University Press, 1938), p. 472.

Page 50:   "greatly impoverish the prayer": C. S. Lewis, *Christian Reflections,* ed. Walter Hooper (Grand Rapids: Eerdmans, 1967), p. 143.

Page 53:   "Who would be welcomed": Frederick Buechner, *Whistling in the Dark* (San Francisco: Harper & Row, 1988), p. 76.

Page 54:   "always a revolutionary": Evelyn Underhill, *Practical Mysticism and Abba,* ed. John F. Thornton and Susan B. Varenne (New York: Vintage, 2003), p. 173.

Pages 54-55: "What Jesus bids us pray": John R. W. Stott, *Christian Counter-*

Culture: The Message of the Sermon on the Mount (Downers Grove, Ill.: InterVarsity Press, 1978), p. 147.

Page 55: "To say day by day": Evelyn Underhill, *The Spiritual Life* (Harrisburg, Penn.: Morehouse, 1955), pp. 82-83.

Page 56: "More things are wrought": Alfred Tennyson, "Morte D'Arthur," line 415.

Interlude

Page 59: Tertullian linked this to: Matthew 6:33. See Tertullian "On Prayer" 6, in *Tertullian, Cyprian, Origen: On the Lord's Prayer,* trans. Alistair Stewart-Sykes (Crestwood, N.Y.: St. Vladimir's Seminary Press, 2004), p. 46.

Chapter 5: Dependent

Page 62: bread for tomorrow: *Epiousios* is to be taken literally, not eschatologically; see C. J. Hemer, "epiousios," *Journal for the Study of the New Testament* 22 (1984): 81-94.

Page 63: "If we prayed this petition": William Barclay, *The Lord's Prayer* (Louisville, Ky.: Westminster John Knox Press, 1998), p. 82.

Page 64: "pray for daily bread": Richard J. Foster, *Prayer: Finding the Heart's True Home* (New York: HarperSanFrancisco, 1992), p. 185.

Page 65: Such prayer assumes: On this, see David P. Nystrom, *James—The NIV Application Commentary* (Grand Rapids: Zondervan, 1997), pp. 225-26.

Page 67: "tell each other stories about Bob": cited in Henri J. M. Nouwen, "A Meal on Top of a Tombstone," *Leadership* 15, no. 3 (Winter 1994): 11.

Page 68: bread from any other quarter: See F. Merkel, "Bread, Daily, Manna," in *The New International Dictionary of New Testament Theology,* ed. Colin Brown (Grand Rapids: Zondervan, 1986), 1:249-51.

Page 71: "When we are praying": C. S. Lewis, *Miracles* (New York: Macmillan, 1960), p. 179.

Chapter 6: Honest

Page 73:   psychological category of sickness: Karl Menninger, *Whatever Became of Sin?* (New York: Hawthorn, 1973).

Page 73:   lust, greed, anger, pride and envy: Steven Schwartz, *The Seven Deadly Sins* (New York: Gramercy, 1997), p. xi.

Pages 73-74: "not an immoral man": Dorothy Sayers, "The Other Six Deadly Sins," *The Whimsical Christian* (New York: Macmillan, 1987), p. 157.

Page 74:   "so forgiveness is for the soul": Andrew Murray, *With Christ in the School of Prayer* (Springdale, Penn.: Whitaker House, 1981), p. 34.

Page 75:   "we fall short of God's perfect holiness": John MacArthur, *Matthew 1—7*, The MacArthur New Testament Commentary (Chicago: Moody Press, 1985), p. 393.

Page 81:   suppressed this clause of the Lord's Prayer: John Chrysostom, cited in William Barclay, *The Lord's Prayer* (Louisville, Ky.: Westminster John Knox, 1998), p. 92.

Page 82:   "God forgives only the penitent": John R. W. Stott, *Christian Counter-Culture: The Message of the Sermon on the Mount* (Downers Grove, Ill.: InterVarsity Press, 1978), p. 149.

Page 82:   "He that cannot forgive others": George Herbert, cited in William H. Willimon and Stanley Hauerwas, *Lord, Teach Us: The Lord's Prayer and the Christian Life* (Nashville: Abingdon, 1996), p. 83.

Page 82:   "Forgive us as we also forgive": Augustine, cited in *Matthew 1-13*, Ancient Christian Commentary on Scripture, New Testament 1a, ed. Manlio Simonetti (Downers Grove, Ill.: InterVarsity Press, 2001), p. 139.

Page 82:   "Nothing makes us so like God": Chrysostom, cited in *Matthew 1-13*, Ancient Christian Commentary on Scripture, New Testament 1a, ed. Manlio Simonetti (Downers Grove, Ill.: InterVarsity Press, 2001), p. 139.

Page 82:   reunion and restoration: Lewis Smedes, *The Art of Forgiving* (New York: Ballantine, 1996), pp. 23-36.

Page 83:   "I forgive you for stealing from me": Desmond Tutu, cited in ibid., pp. 26-27.

Page 84:   "we no longer use the memory": Richard Foster, *Prayer* (New York: HarperSanFrancisco, 1992), p. 187.

Page 85:   forgiving others seventy times seven: C. S. Lewis, *Reflections on the Psalms* (San Diego: Harcourt Brace Jovanovich, 1958), p. 25.

Page 85:   trying to forgive for thirty years: C. S. Lewis, *Letters to Malcolm, Chiefly on Prayer* (New York: Harvest, 1964), p. 106.

Page 85:   person he had at last forgiven: C. S. Lewis, *Letters to an American Lady,* ed. Clyde Kilby (Grand Rapids: Eerdmans, 1967), p. 117.

Chapter 7: Humble

Page 87:   "two equal and opposite errors": C. S. Lewis, *The Screwtape Letters* (New York: Bantam, 1982), p. xiii.

Page 91:   "And then my world broke": Gordon MacDonald, *Rebuilding Your Broken World* (Nashville: Oliver Nelson, 1988), p. 53. It should be noted that MacDonald has been a model of repentance and is fully restored to his wife and family.

Chapter 8: Our Struggle with Unanswered Prayer

Page 98:   God *hears,* God *cares,* God *answers:* The following material first appeared in and has here been adapted and enlarged from the author's *Embracing the Mysterious God* (Downers Grove, Ill.: InterVarsity Press, 2003), pp. 67-77.

Page 101:   The yes we can identify: For more on this, see James Emery White, *You Can Experience a Spiritual Life* (Nashville: Word, 1999), and Bill Hybels, *Too Busy Not to Pray* (Downers Grove, Ill.: InterVarsity Press, 1988).

Page 105:   "otherwise be entirely appropriate and helpful": Dallas Willard, *Hearing God* (Downers Grove, Ill.: InterVarsity Press, 1999), pp. 26-27.

Page 106:   "Very often I was more occupied": Teresa of Ávila, cited by Simon Chan, *Spiritual Theology* (Downers Grove, Ill.: InterVarsity

Press, 1998), p. 137.

Page 108:   "down into the recreating silences": Thomas R. Kelly, *A Testament of Devotion* (New York: Harper & Row, 1941), p. 121.

Page 108:   "My lessons consist of a lot of silence": Bruce Pandolfini, cited in Anna Muoio, "All the Right Moves," *Fast Company,* May 1999, p. 192.

Page 109:   students on the meaning of silence: Kathleen Norris, *Amazing Grace* (New York: Riverhead, 1998), p. 17.

Page 110:   "the Bible uses hearing, not seeing": Frederick Buechner, *Whistling in the Dark* (San Francisco: Harper & Row, 1988), p. 58.

Page 110:   "a place of silence, waiting, and temptation": Alan Jones, *Soul Making: The Desert Way of Spirituality* (New York: HarperSanFrancisco, 1989), pp. 6, 62-63.

A Final Word

Page 111:   "the work of God takes precedence": Esther de Waal, *Seeking God: The Way of St. Benedict* (Collegeville, Minn.: Liturgical Press, 2001), p. 147.

Page 112:   "Prayer . . . is simply a form of waking up": Douglas Steere, *Prayer and Worship* (Richmond, Indiana: Friends United Press, 1978), pp. 12-13.

Page 112:   "God meets man in awful immediacy": Thomas R. Kelly, *A Testament of Devotion* (New York: Harper & Row, 1941), pp. 55-56.

Page 113:   God listens me into silence: see Douglas Steere and Jeanie Crawford-Lee, *Dimensions of Prayer* (Nashville: Upper Room Books, 2002), p. 58.

Page 114:   "How great, dearest brothers": Cyprian "On the Lord's Prayer" 9, in *Tertullian, Cyprian, Origen: On the Lord's Prayer,* trans. Alistair Stewart-Sykes (Crestwood, N.Y.: St. Vladimir's Seminary Press, 2004), p. 70.

Page 114:   inhale the very air of eternity: See Evelyn Underhill, "Breathing the Air of Eternity," *Weavings* 17, no. 3 (May-June 2002).

To learn more about seminars, audiotapes and other resources from James Emery White for the development of your spiritual life as well as the pursuit of a Christian mind, answering the call of God on your life, and aligning yourself strategically with the church, visit **www.serioustimes.com**.